OLD TESTAMENT GRACE

Jon Dybdahl

Pacific Press Publishing Association
Boise, Idaho
Oshawa, Ontario, Canada

Edited by Randy Maxwell
Designed by Tim Larson and Linda Griffith
Typeset in 10/12 Century Schoolbook

Unless otherwise noted, all scriptural references come from the New International Version.

Library of Congress Catalog Card Number: 89-62153

ISBN 0-8163-0877-2

90 91 92 93 94 • 5 4 3 2 1

To Our Parents
Erma Glantz Dybdahl
Gerhardt Lee Dybdahl
and
Jane Breese Trefz
Emanuel E. Trefz
Whose constant love and continued caring first taught us about a gracious God.

Special Acknowledgments
To Walla Walla College and faculty colleagues for providing the environment where books and ideas can be born.
To my department chairman John Brunt for his special encouragement of my writing endeavors.
To Mary Laabs and my wife Kathy for their decipherment of my barely legible scribblings, which they turned into something all can read.

Table of Contents

I

Introduction

The year 1988 marked the 100th anniversary of the year righteousness by faith received special emphasis in the Adventist Church. At such an occasion it is very appropriate to consider that magnificent theme again. Some probably expect such a discussion to follow certain lines. They will probably be disappointed in this book. At the risk of sounding negative, I begin by stating certain things this volume is *not*.

This book is *not* an attempt to solve the theological and historical issues arising out of 1888. I don't propose new insights on the definition of righteousness by faith or the covenant. I neither condemn nor exonerate the church on the basis of its response or lack of response to the 1888 message.

This volume is *not* a book primarily for theologians. If they want to read it, fine, but it is meant not so much to analyze or explain but to comfort and inspire regular people who seek God.

This volume is not exhaustive. It doesn't claim to tell the full story of Old Testament grace but gives examples that are meant to function as a pair of glasses that provide new ways of looking at Scripture. Many of the stories cited are not new. What the book does try to do is cast the old stories and passages in a new light that shows more clearly their power and beauty.

This book does attempt to say that the Old Testament is full of the message of righteousness by faith—of God's grace. This grace is shown in a multitude of ways. Realizing this lets God speak with a unified voice in both testaments and enriches our understanding of righteousness by faith. I repeat the same message over and over in a variety of ways so that this message may sink deep inside.

What this book also tries to do is touch the will and emotions. Through story and appeal, it deliberately sets out to move, inspire, and change the reader. I believe righteousness by faith must be known with the heart as well as the head. For this reason all but the last few chapters end with a story.

What I hope to do is move the whole discussion of righteousness by faith to a new place so that some of the old baggage and argument can be dropped. I hope and pray that in the process people can see with new eyes and react with fresh zeal to the power of the message.

What about a definition of righteousness by faith? I like the definition given by William G. Johnsson, editor of the *Adventist Review*, in the January 7, 1988, special righteousness by faith issue of the magazine, pages 2 and 3. His definition contains four short statements: (1) "Our desperate need," (2) "We cannot help ourselves," (3) "God does for us what we cannot do for ourselves" (this He does freely, unconditionally, and graciously), and (4) "God's grace transforms our entire being." I simply suggest that this understanding of righteousness by faith is the message of the Old Testament as well as the New.

You may ask, "Why are you writing this book?" To ask that question is to ask about me and gives occasion for a story—my story of God's grace.

As Paul was a Pharisee of the Pharisees, I was an Adventist, born and bred. I learned the beliefs I hold dear both at home and at school. Although I have always wondered about some things in the church, I have never felt rebellious or angry. I have never wished for a different upbringing. I have never wanted to be anything but an Adventist. I have always felt that there was something basically right about the things I was taught. I grew up in a loving family and a nurturing community and didn't want it any other way.

I am not sure when the feeling began, but it was quite early. It was a deep uneasiness about the whole religion thing. In those days I understood it basically as a question—*Will I ever make it to heaven?* Or more accurately, *Is there any real hope I will ever make it to heaven?* Somehow, for some unknown reason, the deep parts of me repeatedly said, *It's a long shot, and chances are slim.*

I tried to confess all my sins to God and ask for forgiveness, but it didn't seem to work. At one time I remember making a list of every person I could ever remember wronging and writing a letter asking their forgiveness. I sent money to pay for some oranges I had eaten out of the grove behind our house. In spite of it all, the answer to my question about making it still seemed the same—slim, very slim.

In my later teenage years I managed to suppress the question. It was hard to talk about, and I put it on the back burner. About halfway through my college experience, I switched from the premed course to a theology major. That switch came about, not because of a religious conversion, but for two other reasons. One, I was bored with science and found religion much more interesting and challenging. And, two, a series of amazing events convinced me that God wanted me in theology. Why, I didn't know.

The whole theology program raised the question for me again. Was there any assurance of salvation? I was helped in those years by teachers in college and seminary. Of particular benefit was a class entitled Righteousness by Faith taught by Edward F. Heppenstall. Through him and others I began intellectually to believe and understand God's grace and righteousness by faith. That helped—some. The *mind* was somewhat relieved, but the familiar gut feeling of the *old* worldview remained.

Living in familiar surroundings with no undue pressure made life tolerable in this state. Moving overseas to Asia changed that. The pressures of a new language, culture, climate, and work took their toll and brought out some of the worst in me.

I can remember crying out, "I'm a Pharisee—a Pharisee! I am preaching salvation to others, and yet I don't know salvation for myself." For three or four years, I read and studied all I could about assurance. I talked to my wife Kathy about it, but no one else. I was embarrassed. How could I, as an ordained minister, ask others about these issues on which I was a supposed authority?

In this dark night of long struggle, two things helped. First, I became convinced that God wanted His children to have confidence about their salvation. Second, I took courage that others had tread the same path I was on. John Wesley's biography was a special help. In A. Skevington Wood's biography of Wesley, I reread the section on his conversion numerous times with much underlining.

One early morning in my sweltering Singapore study, I had had enough. Sprawled on the floor in desperation, I told God I was tired—of study, struggle, and uncertainty. Unless He could somehow assure me in my heart of hearts that I was His child, I couldn't go on much longer. Unless my heart could be warmed like Wesley's, my ministry would continue to be dry. I needed a personal, deep assurance that Jesus Christ was indeed *my* Saviour.

In His graciousness, God heard my prayer, and the struggle ended. My heart was strangely warmed. The whole thing dropped the eighteen inches from my head to my heart, and *I was changed.*

This story affects what follows in many ways. First, if it hadn't been for that sultry morning in Singapore, this book would never have been written. This is my feeble attempt at a song of praise for God's grace. Second, I am convinced that simply explaining the issue theologically isn't the whole solution. For many, there is a kind of deep "something" that makes it hard to accept God's grace even when intellectually convinced. There is an attitude or way of looking at things from the place where they really live makes it hard for this liberating truth to be real. One can call this many things—

worldview, life metaphor, emotional/psychological bent, temperament, or whatever, but the attitude is there. At least it was for me, and I suspect it is for others as well. What changes people is not to know the doctrine of righteousness by faith with the head, but to know it with the whole being. This very basic bent of a person must be changed; then the heart can sing. Third, there are a variety of ways to get at the issue—story as well as theology, song as well as proclamation, sermon as well as lesson, symbol as well as poem.

In the pages that follow I attempt to tell the story of God's grace from as many Old Testament angles as I can. I want those who struggle as I did to be moved in heart as well as in mind so the whole being can be affected by God's graciousness. And thus moved, we can all sing in praise for our free salvation.

1

Is God's Personality Split?

People with split personalities confuse us. We never know which side will show itself in any given situation. Is this the "patient" day or the "fly-off-the-handle" day? Will conversation be genteel and calm or heated and acrimonious? We can never know in advance. More predictable people are easier to deal with.

For hundreds of years the Christian church has had a problem dealing with the two parts of its Bible—the Old and New Testaments. In the eyes of many Christians today, God has a split personality—one face of God showing in the Old Testament and the other personality manifesting itself in the New.

The second-century heretic Marcion and his followers believed there were actually two Gods in the Bible. The Old Testament God was a God of law who was contradictory, fickle, ignorant, despotic, authoritarian, and cruel. The New Testament God was a God of love whom Jesus came to reveal. These two Gods had nothing in common. In fact, the purpose of the New Testament God was to overthrow the earlier Old Testament God.

While most Christians rightly reject this view, many still see too great a difference between the two testaments. They reject the two-God idea but do see one God with a real split personality—one who displays a great difference in the way He behaves. This kind of God is hard to deal with.

This split personality of God is portrayed in many different ways. One popular way to split God's personality is by the idea of *dispensation*. In each dispensation—age or period of time—God deals with His people in different ways. God made agreements or covenants with different people in various time periods, and the terms of these covenants are not the same. Some people in earlier ages were saved by doing *works* for God, while people today are saved by God's *grace*.

Certainly God can relate to man in more ways than one, but a person can't help wondering how such a basic thing as salvation could be reached by such divergent paths. Is God really that different?

Other people explain the supposed contradiction by saying the Old Testament is a book of law, and the New Testament is a book of grace. This is a modified version of dispensationalism. Again one wonders why God changed methods. Are modern sinners all that different from sinners of 2,500 years ago? Besides, why does the New Testament itself talk about law and commandments? And why does the Old Testament record that Noah "found grace in the eyes of the Lord"?

Yet another group declares that this is all a matter of progressive revelation. God gave only a partial revelation in the Old Testament—the New Testament is a full revelation of God that completes the picture. This idea isn't bad if the New Testament just builds on the Old Testament, and the same God works in a similar way. The idea has problems when people see the progression as something *totally different*. God is cruel and judgmental in the Old Testament and merciful and loving in the New. Again, God ends up with a split personality.

Christians have always theoretically believed in one Bible

and one God. I believe that the God of the Old Testament is the God of the New Testament, and He is very gracious—much more gracious than most realize! This book is written not only to argue this point logically and theologically but also with the deep conviction that a true recognition of that grace changes people's hearts and lives.

DEFINITION OF GRACE

The definition of grace that I use is simply "unmerited favor." Grace is a free act of God to save and bless. God treats people much better than they deserve, saving them when they have done nothing to merit it. He loves and cares even when they don't. He reaches out to bless even when He is not called upon.

The fact that God does this is the very heart of the Christian message. Many Christians, especially Protestants, call this grace "righteousness by faith," following the terminology of the apostle Paul. Paul teaches that people enter a right relationship with God based on their acceptance by God solely on the grounds of His righteousness and power manifested in Jesus. The gospels teach the same thing using different terminology. People are delivered from sin by simply *receiving* what God in Christ offers freely to those who are totally undeserving. The Bible uses the analogy of gifts and love to explain grace, and the analogy of the legal system to explain righteousness by faith. Different parts of the Bible use different words and analogies, but the concept remains the same.

This should not be amazing. After all, Paul's great exposition of righteousness by faith in Romans is heavily based on the Old Testament. The first four chapters of Romans alone contain eleven Old Testament proof texts. Paul argues righteousness by faith from the Old Testament.

We may call what God does for people through Jesus Christ "righteousness by faith," "redemption," "new birth," "salvation," "deliverance," etc., but the message of them all is the same. God saved, saves, and always will save sinners graciously—based on His love, not on the sinner's actions. The Old Testament teaches this in a clear way and thus speaks with the same voice as the New Testament.

The evidence is found not in a few isolated proof texts, but in the very structure of the Old Testament itself. This grace is heralded in story, ritual, song, and descriptions of God. It is not a minor, secondary theme but an all-pervasive, dominant melody ringing loudly throughout the pages of the Old Testament. Listen carefully as I attempt to play the symphony of grace in the following pages. God is One, and He is very gracious. To know this in the depths of your being will change you and make your heart sing. The song is better heard and understood if played over and over.

A STORY OF GRACE

When he came to my office, he asked a question—or rather a series of persistent questions. The whole process took place politely, but I could tell by the set of his jaw he meant business and would not accept cheap answers.

As an Asian Buddhist on an American Christian campus, he wanted to get to the bottom of things. What was all this stuff about the Bible and Jesus? Did it have any basis in fact? Could you tell anything from history? Since I had been in Asia, he thought I would at least know enough about Buddhism to dialogue. His questions were good ones, and they kept coming. He came back once or twice for further dialogues on evidence, but I knew he really needed something else. He needed to hear about God's grace. The most common saying in Thai Buddhism is *tum di dai di tum chua dai chua*. Roughly translated, it means "Do good, and you receive good—do evil and receive evil." It is a statement of the law of cause and effect, sometimes called "the law of karma." In many ways it makes a lot of sense, but in a theological sense it leaves out grace. The next time he came, I asked him if he'd like to know the heart of the teaching of Jesus—the whole Bible, for that matter. He said Yes. I told him as clearly as I could that God loved sinners and graciously—in both the Old and New Testaments—accepted them. I told him a new saying, *tum chua dai di*. "Those who do evil receive good"—all because of God's grace.

You could see his face change. The determined lines softened; the eyes became intent in looking at mine. A soft light came on his countenance. I asked if he understood. He said, "I'm not sure, but I like it."

"Is this good news?" I asked.

"Yes," he said softly.

He came often after that. I asked if he needed to study Adventist doctrine. "No," he said. He'd had enough classes to understand doctrine. What did he want to hear? "More of the same," he said. "More grace."

The first time or two, I could say some new things. Soon, however, I began to repeat myself. I asked him if he minded. "No," he said, "I like to hear it again and again."

I don't know how many times he came back, probably six or seven. The effect was always the same. He was moved, and so was I. So we together—a Buddhist listening with the heart and a struggling college professor—basked together in the strangely warming light of the grace of God.

Though all the following chapters go by different titles, they are all trying to say something about God's grace. We can all be warmed as we hear it over and over. Come, let us bask together in the strangely warming glow.

What I attempt to do in this book is not to offer new stories, but new ways of looking at old stories. What I have tried to do is give examples that will serve to create a lens through which you can look at the Old Testament in a new way. Once that lens is in place, you can add your own examples and fill out mine. You can help finish telling the story of God's grace.

II

Grace in Old Testament Stories

The narrative or story portion of the Old Testament is the largest part of the book. Stories seem to be God's primary way of communicating with us. While these stories do not often use words like *grace* or terms like *righteousness by faith,* their message speaks vividly and eloquently of the *ideas* contained in those terms. The next three chapters give examples of three major types of stories that tell of God's strength—the story of Israel, stories of Old Testament characters, and stories of Old Testament battles.

2

The Story of Israel

In grade school I hated to make outlines. I was convinced they were part of a plot to keep me doing busy work so I'd have less time to play ball at recess. In my early days in college I followed the same path and generally ignored outlines—both those written by others and my own. I finally awakened in preaching class. It dawned on me that if one had a good outline, the sermon was at least half-written. I learned also that if I had a good outline of a book, I might understand it without having to read it all. If I read the whole book, it made more sense if I had the outline in mind. Outlines were shorthand ways of getting your point across.

Many people have never taken time to think about the general outline and shape of the Bible. They deal only with isolated parts or texts and never look at the broad structure and grasp the basic message. I suggest that the broad structure of the story of Israel speaks loudly of God's love.

The first five books of the Bible that we often call the Pentateuch (five-volume work) were known to the Jews as *Torah* ("law," or better yet, "instruction"). The *Torah* was not five books but *one* book in five sections. This *Torah* was the foundational document of Israel. It was their constitution and charter of existence. Note how it is put together.

The first eleven chapters of Genesis are set in a *world* context. The Creation, Fall, Flood, and Tower of Babel introduce us to God's early dealing with mankind. The rest of the Pentateuch is placed in the context of *Israel*. From Genesis 12 to the end of Deuteronomy—actually the rest of the Old Testament—the story is of Abraham and his family and descendants, the people of Israel. Understanding the key elements in the story of Israel teaches us much about God's grace.

1. *God initiates and continues the whole process*. God came to Abraham and gave him a command and promises (Genesis 12:1-3). Abraham did not seek God, but rather, God found Abraham. By and large the story is one of God seeking Israel. Israel rarely looked for God except when she was in dire straits, like suffering under slavery or persecution.

God not only initiated the process, but also continued it. At the same time, He put Himself on the line for Israel. One of the most moving accounts in all of Scripture is the making of the covenant between the Lord and Abraham in Genesis 15. As a pledge that God would give the land to Abraham's descendants, a deeply meaningful ritual was performed. The Lord told Abraham to bring some animals. With the exception of the birds, they were to be cut in half and laid opposite each other. When the sun set, a smoking firepot with a blazing torch (symbolizing the Lord) passed between the pieces. This seemed to signify that the One passing between the pieces was saying, "May I be cut in half like these animals if I do not keep My pledge." God not only initiated the process but pledged the very integrity of His being to finishing that which He had begun. He was willing to be "cut in half" if He didn't fulfill His promises.

2. *What God proposes to do are good things*. God came to Abraham, and Isaac and Jacob as well, promising blessings. These blessings were for them and all humankind. Note the

promises of Genesis 12:2, 3; 15:1, 5; 17:2-8, 20, 21; 28:13-15. God will bless and multiply and give the land to Israel. All other people will be blessed through them.

In the midst of this constant repetition of promises and blessings in the latter part of Genesis are found few requirements and no codified laws. Only three things seem to be important. One, Abraham must leave Ur for Palestine, and his descendants must stay there. Two, they must worship and stay in contact with God. Three, males must be circumcised.

I am not arguing that the family of Abraham knew no laws. At this time laws were simply not important. What must happen first in the God-man relationship is that God be known as trustworthy—a promise-making and promise-keeping God. That lays the foundation for all that follows.

3. *The people of Israel received God's blessings, not on the basis of merit or good deeds, but on the basis of God's grace.* The story of Abraham's family, especially in the latter part of Genesis, reads like a TV soap opera script. People lied, cheated, fought, fornicated, and had family problems and multiple marriages. They repeat the same sins over and over. It is almost as if they dared God to keep His promises in the face of their sin. The Lord patiently worked through all of their folly and slowly but surely fulfilled His promises.

Not only sin but also everyday problems beset them. A good example of this is the story of the struggle to fulfill the promise that Abraham's descendants would be numerous. That, of course, required children. For the first three generations there were problems of barrenness. Sarah, Rebekah, and Rachel all had fertility problems. The long-looked-for (and necessary) children arrived by God's power and grace in spite of human inability.

These problems were recorded in Scripture, not to glorify the sin or the difficulty, but to contrast human weakness with God's mercy. The humanness of human beings makes the grace of God clear. This is the reason for scriptural honesty.

What the stories imply, other Bible passages make explicitly clear. Nothing in Israel merited God's favor.

It was not her size—God had made Israel whatever she was

anyway! "It was not because you were more in number than any other people that the Lord set his love upon you and chose you, for you were the fewest of all peoples" (Deuteronomy 7:7, RSV).

Clearly, it was not her righteousness. "Not . . . because of your righteousness; for you are a stubborn people." "From the day you came out of the land of Egypt, until you came to this place, you have been rebellious" (Deuteronomy 9:6, 7).

What, then, was the reason? It was a totally nonrational reason—grace and love. "It is because the Lord loves you, and is keeping the oath which he swore to your fathers" (Deuteronomy 7:8).

To say one is chosen because of love may not satisfy curiosity over the reason, but it warms the heart and changes the will. If Israel had been chosen because of size (power, prestige) or righteousness, she could become unchosen and unloved if she became small or unrighteous. Love lasts. The man who professes love for his wife because of her beauty may temporarily satisfy her needs of acceptance and desirability, but sooner or later the question will come, "What about when I'm old?" or "What if there is a disfiguring accident or surgery?" Love based on looks can change, but love for the sake of love and promise lasts. That is the heart of God's grace to Israel.

4. *God remains faithful in spite of the people's unfaithfulness.* Israel's sin in the wilderness ultimately didn't keep them out of Canaan. Israel's rebellion did keep them in Babylonian captivity, but God brought about a new exodus. The unfaithfulness of Israel highlights the faithfulness of God.

All of the above four points make up a good definition of grace. Grace is reaching out and initiating contact. Grace is making good promises—and keeping them! Grace is receiving people, not on the basis of merit, but of love. Grace is remaining faithful when others are unfaithful.

DEUTERONOMY AND THE SEQUENCE OF GRACE

Not only does the story of Israel demonstrate the *fact* of God's grace, a close look can even suggest a *sequence* of how God works in grace with people. While, in my estimation, the whole Pentateuch demonstrates this sequence, it is most clearly seen in the structure of Deuteronomy.

After a brief introduction, Deuteronomy contains the three final sermons of Moses and then a postscript describing his death. What is crucial to note is the organization, the order of Moses' three sermons.

Deuteronomy 1:5 says that Moses' sermons endeavored to explain "this law," referring to all the commands God had given for Israel. What Moses says, however, is not what we would normally think of as law. In chapters 1:6—4:43, Moses recounts the history of the people from Mount Sinai to their present situation. This history clearly makes it known that they were where they were solely because God had been with them and acted on their behalf. He had delivered them. Note these words from the latter part of this same oral history:

> When the Lord your God brings you into the land he swore to your fathers, . . . a land with large, flourishing cities you did not build, houses filled with all kinds of good things you did not provide, wells you did not dig, and vineyards and olive groves you did not plant—then when you eat and are satisfied, be careful that you do not forget the Lord, who brought you out of Egypt, out of the land of slavery (Deuteronomy 6:10-12).

God not only promised more good and gracious things in the future, but also referred them to His graciousness in the past. This graciousness of God in the Exodus must be made clear to future generations when they ask the reason for God's laws and stipulations (see Deuteronomy 6:20-23).

This section, Deuteronomy 6 to 11, repeatedly refers to the Egyptian deliverance and God's other saving acts in Israel's history. Only after these acts are driven home does Moses proceed to the actual laws in chapters 12 to 26.

Following the laws is what I call Moses' final appeal or altar call in which he points out the blessings for following and the curses for not following God. The covenant was renewed. The people were urged to choose God and life rather than death. The future was provided for, and Moses blessed the tribes.

The order here is what is crucial. God's gracious, saving acts for Israel are always proclaimed before the law is presented. In Deuteronomy grace precedes duty, salvation comes before obligation, acts of love are antecedent to laws.

This is the order found throughout the Pentateuch as well! God's promises to Abraham and the Exodus precede Mount Sinai. The Ten Commandments come in Exodus 20, not Genesis 12. They are repeated in Deuteronomy 5 not Deuteronomy 1. Before new commands dealing with the life in Canaan are given, new acts of grace are promised, and past acts of saving grace are remembered. The church can learn from Israel the proper order in which the message of God is to be given!

The very structure, then, of the Pentateuch and Deuteronomy teaches us a very important truth. God always begins in love and grace and saving—not in requiring. The requirements of God can be understood only by those already experiencing the saving grace of God. Only freed slaves can offer the kind of obedience desired by a loving God. The way to win people *back* to obedience is to retell and help them to relive the experience of grace in their lives. The Old Testament story of Israel is clearly a story of grace.

A MODERN STORY OF GRACE

She came up to me quietly after a class I had taught about Old Testament grace at a camp meeting. Although she concealed it well, she was, by her own account, functionally blind. She was approaching 30 years of age and desperately desired a family and children. "Where was this grace you talked about so much *in my life*?" she asked. "How could one who was blind and childless speak of God's saving love?"

My heart ached for her, and I didn't know what to say. Finally, the thought came to me to ask about her life and let her recount her own history. At my request she began to talk. It came slowly at first, trickling from her lips, constricted by the painful memories. Then, as if the telling itself eased the pain, it flowed out in a gushing torrent of words. There had been a painful childhood of alternating abuse and neglect.

Somehow, in her loneliness and search for comfort, she had, through a spirit medium, become friends with a spirit being no one else could see. At first it had been fun, but slowly the being became a nuisance. He would not leave when she said goodbye and made all kinds of demands she resented. She became frightened. To the outward misery she daily experienced was added the inner unseen horror which no one could know. She was a slave.

Then her brother brought her the gospel. She went to church and met loving people and began to sense forgiveness. Eventually she shared with fellow church members the secret of the spirit being, and in a special prayer session, the unwanted companion was sent packing. Friends had brought her to camp meeting and were even now waiting for her as we talked.

"Don't you know what I am going to say?" I asked.

"Yes," she replied. "I guess I had kind of forgotten the story of my life. God has been good. There are many ways His grace has been shown."

The living remembrance of God's grace in the past is probably the surest path to experiencing His continuing grace in the future. If God dealt in grace with Israel—a bunch of unfaithful, hardheaded former slaves—He will certainly deal graciously with us. Retelling the story helps make God's grace a present and living reality.

3

Stories of People

Not only is God's grace amply demonstrated in the history of Israel, it is also clearly seen in the biographies of key Old Testament characters, such as Abraham, Moses, and David.

ABRAHAM

I often tantalize my Old Testament classes by asking them if the Old Testament says anything about the character of Abraham before God called him. The answer is *nothing*. Nothing at all is said about how good (or bad) a person Abraham was. What matters to Genesis is that Abraham responds when the call comes.

Some students are always upset by this. Surely God would choose only a *good* man. Now it may be that *morally* Abraham was the best there was. We don't know, but that is not crucial to the story. In fact, no reason is given in Genesis for the choice of Abraham. The only implied reason may be that he is a descendant of Shem. God's choice is just that—His choice. It is not our choice and is not, according to Scripture, based on merit. God had no "Mr. Righteous Character" contest as a prelude to choosing Abraham.

The Bible records enough stories of Abraham's sins *after* his call to make us realize he was far from perfect. And if, before God chose him, Abraham was anything like he was afterward, his humanity shows very clearly. God called Abraham for what he could become, not as a reward for what he was. God's call, then, is a call of grace—an undeserved invitation that comes to us while we are yet in our sin and humanity, asking us to respond in service to God.

These facts about Abraham's life are crucial because Abraham is such a pivotal character in Scripture. Time and again, what God did for Israel in the Old Testament is said to take place because of the covenant that God made with Abraham. If the covenant God made with Abraham is based on grace, the covenant with Israel must also be based on grace.

In the New Testament, Abraham becomes, for Paul, the key Old Testament demonstration of righteousness by faith. The two central Pauline books defining righteousness by faith and defending the gospel are Romans and Galatians. Both use Abraham as a prime example of the doctrine (see Romans 4 and Galatians 3).

Not only was the initial call of Abraham based on grace, but subsequent key events in his life found their source in God's unmerited favor. The birth of Isaac, the finding of Rebecca as a wife for Isaac, and the preservation of Abraham's family are seen as gifts of God based on His promise, not merit.

One of the interesting incidents of God's preservation *and* grace occurs in Genesis 12. Because of famine, Abraham had to go down to Egypt. He became afraid that the Egyptians would desire to take the beautiful Sarah for a wife and that might lead to his death. As a way out, Abraham convinced Sarah to say she was his sister. Sure enough, based on this story, Pharaoh took her into his house with plans to marry her and gave Abraham much wealth. God saved Sarah (and

Abraham) by bringing disease on Pharaoh's household. Abraham sinned, but God, in His grace, not only saved him, but let him keep all his wealth. Abraham became wealthy through a lie and didn't lose the loot (see Genesis 13:1, 2)!

Abraham became what he was—chosen founder of Israel—on the basis of God's grace.

MOSES

Moses' story is in many ways similar to Abraham's. The only difference is that Moses' story begins earlier in his life. He was miraculously delivered from death and went to live in Pharaoh's house as an adopted child of Pharaoh's daughter. Nowhere is this chain of circumstances attributed to the goodness or righteousness of Moses or his parents.

Moses, like Abraham, as seen in the very first chapter describing his life, committed a serious sin (see Exodus 2). While Abraham lies about his wife, Moses murdered an Egyptian. The reason God delivered Israel was not that He had finally found a righteous man. Rather, it was because the suffering of the people caused God to remember His covenant with Abraham, Isaac, and Jacob.

Forty years in the wilderness herding sheep were needed to prepare Moses for what God had in mind for him. This means that the story of Moses is like that of Abraham. The call of God, the protection of God, and the blessings of God all came by His unmerited favor. Why? *Because God wants to save people.* Personal merit was not a factor in the calling of these two men. In fact, for both, a long period of preparation and learning were necessary to fit these men for real service. These men were heroes of faith and grace—not works.

DAVID

The same story occurs over and over. Abraham and Moses form the pattern for what follows, and David, the famous king of Israel, fits the same mold.

The story of David's anointing is found in 1 Samuel 16. Samuel was led to the home of Jesse in Bethlehem. Seven of Jesse's sons passed in front of Samuel. Jesse felt that one of these seven would be chosen to be the next king in Israel. No, God wanted the youngest, who was out herding sheep—David! In a society that honored the firstborn son, and the older above the younger, David was the least likely candidate. He was so unlikely in man's eyes he was not even asked to be present. However, God does not see as man does (see 1 Samuel 16:7). God picks the least likely so that His *grace* and love may be magnified.

While David doesn't sin immediately (as Abraham and Moses did), in the same chapter describing how he is chosen, his sins are nevertheless probably even better known than those of his predecessors. The most glaring example is his adultery with Bathsheba and subsequent murder of her husband Uriah.

Amazingly, God took this man in all his sin and moral bankruptcy and promised him His love and blessing—not just for then, but forever. And not just to him but to his descendants and dynasty (see 2 Samuel 7:4-16—especially verse 16). What did David do to deserve it? Nothing!

The sweeping promises of 2 Samuel 7 came as David was considering his desire to build a temple for God. Yet the promises of God through Nathan don't mention these intentions as meritorious or the reason for the promises. The reason for it all was simply God's choice to rule Israel. God didn't need a place to live. All He wanted to do was bless David and His people Israel so that they can then bless the world. The promises were not God's response to good deeds and desires to build Him a temple. They sprung from His heart of caring and from His desire to redeem all of mankind.

Though David and his descendants leave a sin-stained history, their problems are never covered up in the biblical record. This is something unique in ancient documents. The reason these failures are honestly preserved is to show that human error doesn't destroy the promise. If the sinner has repented, the promise and the covenant endure in spite of the sin. Because the covenant is based on grace and promise, sin can be frankly revealed. Where sins abound, grace much more abounds. These biblical biographies clearly demonstrate God's abounding grace.

A MODERN STORY OF GRACE

The Friday-evening meeting was over. A group of ministers had just spent an hour and a half talking about the call to ministry from God. One of the men looked intently at me and said, "Is it possible for one who still struggles, is unsure of his direction, and still loves Big Macs to be called by God?" His eyes and body language both said, "I'm very serious about my question." I said in as many ways as I could, "Yes, yes, yes!" You see, the call is based not on what we were and are but on what God's grace can make us. The summons comes from grace. If those called to be *leaders* are so human and yet receive God's call, certainly those who are called to be regular foot soldiers in the heavenly army can base their acceptance on grace.

In Scripture all those who tell of God's call see that call not as an evidence of their goodness but as a testimony to God's kindness. Those who today sense their call should do the same. The fact is that *all* of our personal stories are exactly like those of Abraham, Moses, and David. None of us deserve to be called, but *we were*—in spite of our sin. It is a testimony to His worthiness, not ours.

4

Stories of War

War is terrible. How can it be a teacher of God's grace? The answer is that the best of Israel's battles were the strangest fights you've ever heard about. The worst of Israel's battles sound like regular battles, but these special battles—the times when God does the fighting—are different. Just how different they are becomes apparent as they are studied. Let us examine some of them.

THE EXODUS

After the horrible night which saw the death of all their firstborn, the Egyptians allowed the Israelites to leave Egypt. It didn't take long, however, for Pharaoh and his officials to change their minds. The sudden loss of their entire slave-labor force was more than they could bear. Mustering his army, Pharaoh pursued the Israelites and overtook them as they encamped by the sea.

The Israelites were terrified of the approaching army and

in anger cried out against Moses and God. "Wouldn't it have been better to die in Egypt?" they questioned. Moses responded to the people with a statement that epitomizes the way Israel's battles were meant to be fought.

> Do not be afraid. Stand firm and you will see the deliverance the Lord will bring you today. The Egyptians you see today you will never see again. The Lord will fight for you; you need only to be still (Exodus 14:13, 14).

Think about this amazing passage, for it lays the pattern for all the "wars of the Lord." Note first Israel's part. Nothing is said about fighting or weapons or battle. It doesn't say, "Fight, and God will help you because you are helping yourselves." No, Israel was to stop being afraid and to stand still. She was to do nothing but stand and watch God do it.

What was the Lord's part? He fought. The theology of the wars of the Lord is simple. God does it all! The people stand and watch. The deliverance comes through God's grace alone. The enemy is totally destroyed, not because of what the people do but because of what God does. The result of this kind of battle can only be praise to God. You can't praise the army or the generals, when they had nothing to do with the victory. God alone deserves the glory.

The Exodus follows this same pattern. After the Egyptian army drowned in the sea, Israel sang a song of praise to Yahweh.

> I will sing to the Lord, for he is highly exalted. The horse and its rider he has hurled into the sea. The Lord is my strength and my song; he has become my salvation. He is my God, and I will praise him (Exodus 15:1, 2).

Miriam, Moses' sister, led the women in the same song, and with dance and tambourine, the women praised the God who graciously delivers.

This is the way God wants to operate for Israel. The closer she stayed to Him, the less actual fighting she did. When she wandered from her gracious Lord, the more she had to do of the actual fighting. The more Israel fought, the more likely she was to lose the battle! The more dependence there was on God, the more sure the victory.

Story after story in the Old Testament illustrates this principle. I tell three more of them because they are so interesting and because they all have a different twist. In each, Yahweh operated uniquely. He didn't work by different principles but in each case did something wild and crazy in order to make it clear beyond the shadow of a doubt that He alone won the victory—not man. I think these stories also represent God's sense of humor. I suspect He was tempted to smile at what happened.

THE AMALEKITES

The Israelite defeat of the Amalekites is recorded in Exodus 17:8-16. The Amalekites attacked an ill-prepared Israel. Moses told his assistant Joshua to pick "some of our men" and go fight the Amalekites. He also added, "I will stand on top of the hill with the staff of God in my hands."

The next day Joshua took his chosen group of men to fight while Moses and two assistants climbed the nearby hill. As long as Moses held up his hands with the rod of the Lord, Israel won. When he lowered his hands, the Amalekites prevailed. When Moses's hands tired, his assistants, Aaron and Hur, got a rock for him to sit on, and then each held up one of his arms. Israel won.

After the Lord's command to record in writing the story of the battle, Moses built an altar. He called this altar "The Lord is my banner." A banner or standard was often used to rally an army (see, for instance, Psalm 60:4). The implication here is clearly that the Lord Himself is the Standard around which Israel rallies. He is the One who brings victory. Moses's altar honored the God who wins battles simply through uplifted hands and a rod.

GIDEON

The story of Gideon and the Israelite victory over the Midianites is one of the most intriguing stories in the Bible.

All phases of the story illustrate that the great deliverance that takes place comes from the gracious hand of God alone. You may enjoy reading the story in Judges 6 and 7.

Gideon himself does not seem to have been a particularly outstanding person. He described himself as coming from the weakest clan in the tribe of Manasseh and being the least one in his family. How could he save Israel (see Judges 6:15)? In Judges 6:12, the angel of the Lord calls him a "mighty warrior." Those words are either uttered tongue in cheek or are a statement of faith about what comes in the future, for the rest of the chapter seems to illustrate the slowness and weakness of Gideon's faith. First he raised all kinds of questions about his calling and the reality of the angel who appeared before him. Only after a long dialogue and the angel's burning of his offering did he really believe that God had come to him.

The Lord told him to tear down his father's altar to Baal. Fearing reprisals, Gideon tore down the altar at night so no one would see him. His father intervened to save him from the anger of his fellow villagers over the incident.

The Spirit of the Lord came on Gideon, and he summoned Israel to follow him, and warriors came. Even then, Gideon became nervous and had to put a wool fleece out, not once but twice to see if God was really with him. Just before the battle, Gideon seemed fearful again. God strengthened him by causing him to overhear one of the enemy soldiers declaring that, through a dream, he knew God had given the camp of the Midianites and their allies into Gideon's hands.

Books that celebrate victories of the armies of modern nations today would hesitate to tell such a frank story that openly reveals the doubts and fears of their commanding officer. Clearly, this battle was different. It glorified Yahweh, not a general or an army.

Not only is Gideon's condition a statement of God's grace but so is the method of battle. Gideon began with 32,000 men. But by two deliberate actions, the size of the army was reduced to 300. The Lord clearly says that this was so Israel would not boast that she won in her own strength (see Judges 7:2). The final size of Israel's army was so small that God is clearly seen to be the deliverer.

This element is further strengthened by the description of the strange "weapons" these 300 soldiers were to use. All they took to battle were trumpets and empty jars with torches inside. The 300 surrounded the enemy camp, sounded their trumpets, broke their jars, waved their torches, and shouted. The enemy troops in confusion began fleeing and killing each other. A huge mop-up operation followed this great delivering victory.

It is also important to note that the Israelites did *not* deserve this victory because of their righteousness. They had become slaves to the Midianites because of their sin. Things had gotten so bad that they cried out to the Lord for help (see Judges 6:6). As a result, the Lord sent them a prophet. The prophet's words are interesting (see Judges 6:8-10). The message tells of God's great deliverance of Israel in the Exodus and subsequent command not to worship other gods. Israel had not obeyed God's word.

Nowhere does this story tell of Israel's goodness or even repentance as a prerequisite for God's deliverance through Gideon. The only thing needed was the cry for help. Even the leader Gideon had to be specifically told to get rid of the Baal images in his own household. His later life was not always exemplary (see Judges 8:17, 30, 31). The salvation came based solely on God's grace and man's desperate cry for help. The salvation came before repentance and change. *After* the deliverance, Israel seems to have served God—but even that was temporary (see Judges 8:33-35). In the Old Testament story, righteousness was never a prerequisite for deliverance. Need was the only condition. Time and again in the book of Judges, God delivered the Israelites graciously and fully even though they strayed from Him numerous times. What a gracious God!

JEHOSHAPHAT AND THE MOABITE COALITION

King Jehoshaphat panicked when he heard about the vast army of Moabites, Ammonites, and Meunites that was coming against his nation (see the story in 2 Chronicles 20). He gathered all Judah to the temple and prayed for deliverance—confessing Judah's lack of power and the contrasting power of God.

In the assembled multitude the Spirit moved a Levite named Jahaziel to prophesy. Note his words—

> Do not be afraid or discouraged because of this vast army. For the battle is not yours, but God's. . . . You will not have to fight this battle. Take up your positions; stand firm and see the deliverance the Lord will give you, O Judah and Jerusalem. Do not be afraid; do not be discouraged. Go out to face them tomorrow, and the Lord will be with you (2 Chronicles 20:15-17).

These words clearly echo the Lord's message through Moses at the Exodus. The same God deals in the same way with His needy people when they cry out to Him.

Jehoshaphat bowed his face to the ground and, along with all the Israelites, worshiped God. The choir praised God with a loud voice. This was the response to God's gracious promise of deliverance.

Early the next morning Israel went to battle. The whole procedure was crazy—*the choir went first*! They praised God for the splendor of His holiness as they sang, "Give thanks to the Lord, for his love endures forever" (2 Chronicles 20:21).

The Lord set ambushes against the invading army, and they fought among themselves. When the Israelites came over the hill and looked down, the Scripture says, "They saw only dead bodies lying on the ground; no one had escaped" (2 Chronicles 20:24). It took three days to collect the loot, and then began another round of praise! Once again it is abundantly clear that the victory was Yahweh's and Yahweh's alone.

CONCLUSION

Perhaps it would help us to grasp how bizarre all of this is if we put it on a modern context. Imagine a class in battle strategy at West Point Military Academy. Uniformed cadets all march in to class and are introduced to a guest lecturer who promises three sure-fire ways to win a battle.

Method no. 1 is the Moses strategy. During the fighting, you get the president of the United States to hold a Bible in his uplifted hands as he watches the battle from some vantage point. If he gets tired, call on the secretaries of state and defense to hold his arms up. As long as his arms remain aloft, the United States will win.

Method no. 2 is the Gideon way. Pick the most unlikely general you can—one from a small family on the wrong side of the tracks who has a fearful, negative attitude. Put him in charge. Reduce your standing army by more than 90 percent. Do away with all weapons and give the men musical instruments and flashlights. Surround the enemy at night. Play your instruments, turn on your flashlights, and holler about God and your chicken-hearted general. The enemy will become confused and kill each other and flee. You are sure to win.

Method no. 3 is the Jehoshaphat plan. Gather everybody in church and let the president lead in a prayer confessing the utter weakness of the country. Believe the prophecy that comes that says you will be saved. Then gather a choir—maybe the Mormon Tabernacle Choir—and let them take the front lines singing praises to God. The enemy will be defeated.

The teacher of such principles would be laughed off campus or sent to a psychiatric ward.

I can't help but think God enjoyed this a bit. I must laugh as I think about it. By all normal standards these battles and these methods are ridiculous. They seemed as silly to the Israelites as they seem to us today. Their very silliness is testimony to the fact that they work only because of God's action—His gracious delivering. Their humor is eloquent testimony to undeserved salvation that comes by no effort or merit of the Israelites but simply because they cry out to God in their need.

A STORY OF GRACE

We desperately needed a bulldozer to grade roads and

make building sites for our proposed school in the foothills outside Chiang Mai, Thailand. Funds were scarce, and the only available bulldozer we knew of was thirty-five miles away. The cost of transporting it was prohibitive and far above our available money. Lacking normal methods, we began to pray for a bulldozer. We were ready to start building but couldn't do anything on the hilly school property without a bulldozer to level it.

One day soon afterward, I had been to the school property checking on the situation. When the time came to travel back to town, the district headman asked for a ride in our Land Rover, and I gladly complied.

Rounding a corner on the gravel road leading to the main highway, we were flagged to a stop. Men were working on putting in a culvert where one had washed out during the last rainy season. We joined the line of cars awaiting the completion of the work. Shortly after I turned off the motor, I heard a roar in the distance. Nothing was visible, but the sound of a racing motor was coming from behind us. Soon a rapidly moving Jeep came around the corner. I knew he would never get stopped in time. He hit the back end of our Land Rover with a sickening thud.

Several people, including the shaken young driver, emerged from the vehicle. The youthful age of the driver and the stricken look on his face told me something was wrong. He had no driver's license and was not supposed to be driving the Jeep. One of the passengers said, "Guess you'll just have to arrest him."

"Wait a minute," I said. As I walked around the Jeep, I noticed an insignia and the words *Government Land Co-op* painted on the door. Suddenly the light dawned. The Land Co-op! They had a bulldozer! I wondered if they would trade several days of bulldozer use for the repair of a Land Rover.

Appropriate, discreet contacts through intermediaries were made, and the deal was sealed. If I would repair my Land Rover and feed the bulldozer operator, the equipment was available to us. The Rover looked worse than it really was. Chiang Mai was blessed with skilled auto-body men who worked their miracles cheaply. As I remember, it cost me between $30 to $40 to fix. The operator's meals for four days cost about $25. For about $60 we got all of our roads and building sites made! The school is built today on land cleared by that bulldozer.

While receiving a bulldozer is not as crucial as deliverance from your enemies in battle, the principle is similar. Every time I think of the incident, I laugh, and I think God does too. God delights in delivering people in strange ways so that His name may be glorified.

III

Grace in Institutions, Rituals, and Symbols

Not only is righteousness by faith demonstrated in the stories of the Old Testament, it is also portrayed in the rituals, instructions, and symbols of the Old Testament. The next seven chapters endeavor to show how this is true. This can enrich our understanding of grace in the Old Testament and also encourage us to have a greater appreciation of ritual and symbol that is often forgotten in Western Christendom.

5

Sanctuary and Temple

Many modern Christians have a hard time understanding the Old Testament Israelites' adoring love for their sanctuary and temple. For us it smacks of idolatry and represents an old view that ties God to a building or place. We believe God can be worshiped anywhere, and the whole idea of a temple is offensive. While it is true that the temple's meaning and purpose was often distorted by the Jews, it nevertheless has much to teach us. This is best understood by comparing the temple to a modern-day counterpart.

THE OLD TESTAMENT SANCTUARY

The place of central worship used by the Israelites during their wilderness wanderings was called the *tabernacle* or *sanctuary*. The basic function of the tabernacle was clearly stated. It was the place where the presence of God among them was manifested (see Exodus 25:8). God was there and could be communed with at that place.

We must not think that Israel believed the sanctuary service was automatic and that the building alone was significant. When the building was finished, God's glory had to fill it (see Exodus 40:33, 34). The same is true of Solomon's temple (see 1 Kings 8:10, 11). Without the cloud of the presence and the Shekinah glory, the building was not the place of God's presence.

Since the portable sanctuary, and, later, the temple were where God dwelt, they were the places where people came to meet God with praise, petitions, and worship. They were the places where people could gather to meet in times of national emergency and expect God to hear their prayers (see 2 Chronicles 20:8, 9). To celebrate in the sanctuary or the temple meant to celebrate in God's presence.

Since Yahweh is a gracious and delivering God, to have His presence was wonderful and helpful. The temple, by extension, symbolized in a tangible way the religious identity of the Israelites. It showed who they were and who their God was and provided for the ongoing practice of their faith. It is no wonder, then, that David desired to build the temple; it would have been a privilege to do so. The people rejoiced greatly when Solomon completed the temple.

Rebuilding the temple after its destruction by Babylon was the prime task of returning Israelite exiles. They needed their sense of God's presence and religious identity more than anything else. No wonder God, through Haggai and Zechariah, made the rebuilding of the temple a top priority.

By God's living with His people and providing them a way to meet Him and receive His gracious gifts, we see how the temple symbolized God's grace. This is what made the temple a most wonderful place.

One of the most chilling and riveting stories in the Old Testament tells of the departure of God's presence from the temple before the Exile. Ezekiel portrays it as the glory of the Lord leaving the temple (see Ezekiel 10; 11:22-25). First the cloud presence left the mercy seat above the ark in the Most Holy Place and then moved to the threshold of the temple. It hovered at the east gate of the Lord's house and then left

Jerusalem, stopping above the mountain to the east of the city. The horror such a vision evoked in the heart of the Israelites was unspeakable. With God gone, everything was lost. Sure enough, in a short time, city, temple, and nationhood were gone. God's presence in the temple was a gracious gift. His absence brought on unspeakable horrors.

MODERN TEMPLES

Certainly modern church buildings are not equivalent to the temple either historically or practically. They are based on a synagogue model, not the temple model. Also churches that are destroyed can be rebuilt. The loss of a church building is mourned, but the selfhood of its members isn't lost.

Probably the best contemporary comparison to the temple would be the denomination. Loss of the temple would be like a Catholic suddenly realizing God had left Catholicism. The hierarchy and sacraments would lose their power, and no divine presence would remain. It would be like Protestants suddenly finding out that God was gone. Their "protest" would be worthless and their creeds and confessions empty because the Spirit of God had departed. It would be like Adventists discovering that God had gone. They would no longer be His remnant people, and their cherished beliefs, reforms, and end-time messages would be void of the indwelling Christ. Their structure and organization would be irrelevant—doomed.

RESTORATION

The hope of Israel was in restoration. After the exile, the temple was rebuilt. The same Ezekiel who saw the glory depart the temple saw a rebuilt temple as the major element in a restored Israel. This restored temple was bigger, better, and more alive with God's presence than any temple had ever been before (see Ezekiel 40–43). The climax to this jubilant scene occurred when the glory that had departed earlier returned and filled the temple (see Ezekiel 43:1-5). As a result the entire restored city of Jerusalem was to be called "The Lord is there" (Ezekiel 48:35).

The Lord had, in gracious mercy, returned to the temple.

He was there, and His presence made everything right. The temple then was a picture of grace, a place where a loving God dwelt in the midst of His people and ministered to them.

This concept of the temple or tabernacle symbolizing God's presence in the midst of His people finds expression in the gospel of John, chapter 1:14: "The Word became flesh and lived for a while among us. We have seen his glory, the glory of the one and only Son, who came from the Father, full of grace and truth."

The Greek for "made his dwelling" ("lived for a while" in the version quoted above) is connected with the word for tent or tabernacle. Jewish readers would have immediately connected this phrase with the Israelite sanctuary, which was filled with the glory of God (see Exodus 40:34, 35). God's gracious gift of a sanctuary and a tabernacle was the gift of His presence—a marvelous gift indeed.

A STORY OF GRACE

Although I thought the class would consist of only theology majors, I was wrong. Nothing I could say about the course at registration time persuaded her that she should take something else, so I took her in. What a help she proved to be. The vibrant enthusiasm for her newfound faith in Christ was contagious and gave the sometimes-stunned theology majors something to think about.

Several weeks into the quarter, in the calm of my office, she shared the story of how it all began. She was raised in an unbelieving home. Christianity and its stories were not part of her growing up. Consequently, stories she told about strange occurrences in her house were dismissed by her parents as childish nightmares. The same frightening presence she experienced also effected her siblings. They often huddled together at night in fear. In the early years, she could at least escape it at school or at the homes of friends, but eventually the evil presence followed her wherever she went. In the end, she went to college in another country—partly just to get away from whatever was harassing her.

One night, in despair over the whole problem, she had a

dream. In the dream, she saw the communion elements—the bread and grape juice. She didn't know what they were, but she felt a peace and a new loving presence that she had not known before. She wondered what the whole thing meant. Weeks later she shared her dream with friends who were devout Christians. They told her about Jesus, who was "God with us," and the communion symbols of His presence. Obviously her first communion was a powerfully moving experience. She knew that God through His Son had graciously come to be with her, and that Presence meant love and peace and deliverance. God's presence had come to free and be with her—not because of anything that she had done but because of His amazing grace.

6

Sacrifices, the Priesthood, Rituals, and Feasts

If it is hard for modern people to relate to the concept of a temple, they find it even more difficult to relate to sacrifices. Reading the description of animal sacrifices in the books of the Old Testament is, for many people, a difficult experience. These bloody accounts reek with gore and cruelty. For animal lovers, the thought of hundreds of sweet, gentle fluffy lambs going to their deaths each year is hard. Besides this, many things that were commonplace in Israel would have been illegal nowadays for anyone not working in a slaughterhouse or butcher shop. But beyond the revulsion we feel over cruelty to animals, for some there is something even more offensive. This involves the concept of God, which some see implied in the sacrifices. Why does God require blood from innocent animals to forgive people? Why can't He simply forgive people when they confess? Why does all this blood have to be shed? How in the world is sacrifice related to God's grace?

SACRIFICES

To begin the discussion of sacrifice, we need to look at the positioning of the main laws concerning sacrifice in the Old Testament. Laws concerning sacrifice occur in the books of Exodus, Leviticus, Numbers, and Deuteronomy. The largest grouping of these laws, comprising the core of the sacrificial system, however, is found in the book of Leviticus.

To understand these laws, we need to look at their position. In the Pentateuch, the book of Exodus is the book of deliverance. It begins by telling the story of Israel and her deliverance from Egyptian slavery by the mighty arm and outstretched hand of Yahweh, her God. We've already alluded to that story in an earlier chapter.

After the deliverance, God made a covenant with Israel. Following His giving of the covenant and its conditions, God led out in the building of the sanctuary. This tent of meeting, a temporary temple, if you please, served as Israel's place of worship. At the conclusion of the book of Exodus, this temple or sanctuary is dedicated, and the glory and presence of God fill it.

Immediately after that, we have the book of Leviticus. Leviticus describes how the sanctuary or temple functioned. Its aim was to enable people to maintain a relationship with God and continue God's presence in that sanctuary.

The book begins with God living in His house, but it assumes that people are going to sin and go astray. The various sacrifices and ceremonies were instituted to allow God to maintain His presence in the temple and His relationship with the people. The giving of the sacrificial system, then, was an act of grace. Not only did God dwell there in the sanctuary, but through the sacrifices, He provided the means for keeping His presence there and for keeping His relationship with the people alive.

What function does sacrifice play, then? It is simply the practical working out of the relationship that enables God and man to be together.

Many people have attempted to define the meaning of sacrifice. There are numerous ideas and theories about the specific function of sacrifice. I believe that it is hard to pin down the purpose and function to one major idea. If you study the Old Testament, you find that the purposes of sacrifice in the temple varied. They certainly contributed to worship. Some people used sacrifice to worship God and to demonstrate their devotion. In other places, sacrifices were clearly made for the purpose of thanksgiving, of praising God and telling Him how much the people appreciated His blessings and what He had done for them. At times the sacrifices showed commitment or were done in connection with vows that people had made. Sometimes sacrifice was simply demonstrating fellowship—man and God in close relationship. People ate the sacrifices and celebrated in the presence of God and sensed His nearness.

The function of sacrifice that probably interests us most, however, is the function of atonement and cleansing. Sacrifices were the means by which God got rid of sin, forgave people, and allowed them to be cleansed.

Why did God do it this way? Why did sacrifices have to be made? There are, I believe, three major reasons. One, sacrifices were symbols and object lessons, which demonstrated a religious reality. By involving the whole person physically and emotionally in the action that took place, truths beyond mere words were taught. This strengthened the impact of the teaching.

Not only did they symbolize religious realities and relationships with God, the sacrifices also represented for the people who gave them, enormous economic sacrifices. In a pastoral society where animals were the source of wealth, sacrificing an animal to God at the temple was a financial offering.

For people who are used to killing animals, the concept that this was somehow a repulsive experience for the Israelites is, in most cases, exaggerated. I lived for years in Thailand among animistic tribal people who killed animals fairly regularly for food and for sacrifice. I sensed among those people none of the sensibilities that exist in our society regarding killing animals. To them it was either sustenance or the giving of a big offering.

There is a third major role that sacrifice plays. The visual and tangible nature of sacrifice gave the people an assurance that sin was really taken care of—that they could leave it behind them and move on. Our modern society has, generally speaking, lost this aspect of tangibleness. Today, because of the true sacrifice of the Lamb of God, we can approach God in silent prayer and simply ask for His forgiveness. We believe we are forgiven, not based on some visible or tangible manifestation, but by faith—because God *promised* to forgive, and we believe Him. However, it is also appropriate at times to respond to the Spirit of God in a tangible way, such as at an altar call. God doesn't need us to stand or come forward for special prayer in order to grant our requests. But there are times when we may need to experience that special closeness to God that comes when a physical and tangible commitment is made in a public setting. Baptism and the communion service are other examples of this. Both are outward acts symbolizing an inward change of heart and life.

Some have raised the objection that sacrifices were a form of hocus-pocus or primitive magic. Others say they gave rise to a religion based, not on the heart, but on some outward compliance to an empty ritual. That simply was not true in Israelite sacrifices. In Israelite sacrifice, the worshiper had a key role. This is clearly seen in the order of sacrifice recorded in Leviticus chapter 1. The worshiper was to bring the sacrifice. The worshiper placed his or her hand on the animal. The bringer of the offering slaughtered and skinned the animal and cut it in pieces. This same layperson washed the inner parts and the legs. In other words, the worshiper performed the majority of the functions connected with the sacrifice. The symbolism is not that of some priest doing a magical act on the worshiper's behalf. The individual himself had a key part in what happened, and the symbolism involved was a part of his life—it was his animal, his hands upon the animal, and his action. Beyond that, the first part of Leviticus, which contains the core of the sacrificial system, talks about the offerings from the viewpoint of the worshiper or the offerer, not from the viewpoint of the priests.

The Lord called to Moses and spoke to him from the tent of meeting and told him to speak to the Israelites, not the priests, about the sacrifices.

Additionally, many texts specifically state and others imply that confession preceded sacrifice. Sacrifice was not a magic ritual that cleansed sin, but rather a follow-up to confession and repentance. Leviticus 5:5, 6 makes that clear:

> When anyone is guilty in any of these ways, he must confess in what way he has sinned and, as a penalty for the sin he has committed, he must bring to the Lord a female lamb or goat from the flock as a sin offering; and the priest shall make atonement for him for his sin.

Numbers 6:2-6 makes it clear that not only was the worshiper to confess to God, but he was also to confess to others who had been wronged and even make restitution for his deeds when necessary.

The sacrificial system involved the worshiper and his confession and action. It was not something automatic. The whole system was a gracious gift of God enabling people to become emotionally involved in God's plan of eliminating sin, and to fellowship with Him.

THE PRIESTHOOD

Special persons were needed to facilitate and oversee the sacrifices and offerings. The sanctuary also had to be maintained. This was the reason for the priests and Levites. They were gifts God gave to the people, so that the needed work of maintaining the relationship with Him could take place.

At the conclusion of the long process of ordination and cleansing for the priests, an interesting event occurred (see Leviticus 9:23, 24). Moses and Aaron entered the tent of meeting, and when they came out, they blessed the people, and the glory of the Lord appeared to all the people. Fire came down from the presence of the Lord and consumed the burnt offering and the fat portions on the altar. When all the people saw it, they shouted for joy and fell face down. Moses and Aaron and the priests were ordained; they were cleansed. They could then bless the people. The gift of these priests to Israel was an act of God's grace. They were the instruments of God for blessing the people. They made sure the sacrifice took place properly and helped mediate God's forgiveness to the people.

The people understood them clearly as their representatives. It was not the priests who laid their hands on the Levites, but the Israelites themselves in Numbers 8 ordained the Levites and designated them as their representatives. Notice again the function of the Levites and the response of the people. Numbers 8:19 says:

> I have given the Levites as a gift to Aaron and his sons from among the people of Israel, to do the service for the people of Israel at the tent of meeting, and to make atonement for the people of Israel, that there may be no plague among the people of Israel in case the people of Israel should come near the sanctuary (RSV).

As God's gift to the people, the Levites performed the work in the tent of meeting for the Israelites, made atonement for the Israelites, and kept the plagues away. They were God's gift to Israel.

RITUALS AND FEASTS

A few words should be said in connection with the other rituals and feasts of Israel beyond the sacrifices which we have spoken about already.

The climax of Israel's ritual year was the Day of Atonement. It was indeed a solemn time. It seems to have been the only stipulated regular fast day in the Old Testament. We also have a long tradition of connecting the Day of Atonement with judgment. Too often, however, we overemphasize the solemnity of this day. We need to remember what its end results were. Its aim was atonement, which resulted in the total cleansing of the temple or tabernacle and of the people. So the conclusion of that day was joy, cleansing, and salvation.

If one studies the rituals and feasts of Israel, one discovers again that they are symbols of grace. While the mechanics and aesthetics of the system may be offensive to us, one must say in conclusion that for the Israelites, they were loved and cherished. The sacrifices filled a wide range of spiritual and emotional needs. True, the prophets often criticized the sacrifices of those with unconsecrated hearts, but they were not in opposition to this God-ordained system. Israel, because their hearts weren't right, often misused and perverted this system but that cannot negate the evidence that the Israelites loved the sacrificial services. Time and again, the Psalms exclaim something like this: "I will go to the altar of God, to God my exceeding joy" (Psalm 43:4, RSV). Or again, "Blessed is he whom thou dost choose and bring near, to dwell in thy courts! We shall be satisfied with the goodness of thy house, thy holy temple" (Psalm 65:4, RSV). The Israelites loved to go to the temple and partake in the sacrifices that assured them of God's presence there. If the sacrifices were properly used with confession and the human response, their symbolism had a powerful and continuing effect on the Israelites. We can learn from them as well.

A STORY OF GRACE

They had planned a special outing in the mountains during the summertime for a group of rough inner-city kids, their pastor told me. They thought the mountains, a lake, and some trees would be things these kids would enjoy after pounding asphalt streets and baking in the hot summer sun. But these city youths had never experienced nature in this way before. All they wanted to do was stay inside, play games, listen to music, and dance. After a day or two, the counselors and the camp leaders were totally frustrated. They were just about to pack everything up and take the kids home when someone suggested that they try one last thing. They decided that the leaders and counselors would wash all the campers' feet. So, that evening they gathered the youths around and briefly told the story of how Jesus washed the disciples' feet. They began to wash the feet of these kids.

At first it became deathly quiet. Before long, the muffled sound of sobbing and weeping came from the corner of the room. It was not long before all the young people in the room were weeping. The powerful symbol of their leaders washing their feet had moved them when all the words in the world had not been able to.

Symbol and ritual change all of us. For Israel, the sacrifices were powerful symbols of a God who provides the way to come back in contact with Him—a God who cleanses and forgives. Such symbols can continue to teach us about His grace.

7

God's Gracious Law

As already mentioned, many Old Testament practices, rituals, institutions, and concepts are hard to grasp because of the cultural differences involved. The two areas that we have just discussed, the temple and sacrifice, provide examples of this. Law is another example. Law, however, can cause us more trouble because we think we know about laws.

Temples and sacrifices are clearly foreign to our culture, but we do have laws and are familiar with concepts of justice. The problem is that the concept of law in our culture is radically different from concepts of law in Israelite culture.

In our culture, people generally have a negative attitude toward law. Law is seen as unpleasant and bothersome, something that catches us, an entity that points out our sin and shortcomings. In contrast, the Old Testament reveals how Israel deeply loved the law (see, for example, Psalm 119:97, 113, 163).

Nowhere in the Old Testament is law seen as a burden. The psalmist says, "My soul is consumed with longing for your laws at all times" (Psalm 119:20). "Be gracious to me through your law," says Psalm 119:29.

Law is a channel of God's grace—a gracious gift from Him to His people. Anyone who doubts the truth of this statement needs only to read Psalm 119, the longest chapter in the Bible, which is one long hymn of praise to God for His law. Why is this so? Why does the Old Testament present such a favorable picture of God's law? What follows is an attempt to answer this question:

DEFINITION OF LAW

One of the reasons we misunderstand Old Testament law is that we do not understand how broad and deep the concept is. A better translation for the term *law* (Hebrew—*Torah*) would be "instruction" or "guidance." When an Old Testament Israelite heard the term *law*, he usually thought of Moses and the law that Moses gave. By the time of the New Testament, the term *law* referred specifically to what we call the Pentateuch, or the first five books of the Bible—Genesis, Exodus, Leviticus, Numbers, and Deuteronomy. This portion of the Bible certainly contains much more than specific laws and statutes. It contains stories of people, their lives, their sin, but above all, the story of God's people, Israel, and the salvation He worked for them.

This section of the Bible also contains explanations of and instruction for the rituals, institutions, and ceremonies of Israel. For the Israelite, the breadth of meaning in the term *law* is demonstrated very well in Deuteronomy 1:5, where it says that "Moses began to expound this law, saying . . ." That verse introduces the rest of the book, or at least the first sermon in the book. Interestingly, following that introduction comes a history of Israel, which describes the promise that God gave, God's deliverance of Israel, and their experiences with Him leading up to their present situation.

Old Testament law, then, is the telling of history. Law is all of God's instructions—history, ritual, and ceremony, as well as regulations. This law, of course, contains the great salvation of the Exodus and the call of Abraham, as well as all of the commands that we now associate with law. This law also contains the sacrificial guidelines. So, the law that tells people how to live before God also tells how to get rid of the sin that results from ignoring those instructions. The same law that tells of salvation and gives requirements also tells of the way to get right with God when those requirements are not met. This concept of law is much broader and deeper than our idea of specific commands and rules that are usually seen as negative.

THE ROLE OF LAW

Law, then, is a guide for living and believing. It is God's gracious gift that tells people how to live before Him.

I recently purchased a word-processing program for my computer. I know very little about computers and even less about word processing, so I am extremely thankful for the thick instruction manual that came with the word-processing program. In fact, those disks that contain the program would be basically worthless to me without that manual to tell me how to work it. Also listed is a toll-free number that I can call if I have particular problems. This allows me to get in touch with someone who can give me further instructions. You'll never find me complaining about this instruction manual or the toll-free number that it lists or the people who are there to give me help.

Israel viewed law in this way. They had been granted God's free salvation. They stood as His people, but they needed help in knowing how to live. Coming from slavery in Egypt, the habits that had been formed there, the problems that they faced, and the lack of guidance that they had undergone were now remedied by a gracious God who told them how life should be lived. They rejoiced in the instruction and used it, even as I rejoice in and use my computer manual and toll-free number.

Further, *law was never a means of salvation for Israel.* It was help in living life. It was a way of belonging, but it was never the path to a relationship with God.

Even if we were to separate the Ten Commandments from

this total package of "law" or instruction, these were still never seen as a burden or a means of salvation. They were gracious instructions to delivered people.

This is most easily seen by looking at the two passages in the Bible where the Ten Commandments occur—Exodus 20 and Deuteronomy 5. Both of these commandment passages are preceded by the lengthy story of God's deliverance. The first part of Exodus, of course, tells of the deliverance from Egyptian slavery. And in Deuteronomy, the first few chapters preceding the Ten Commandments talk about Israel's experience after the Exodus, and the various ways God saved Israel by defeating her enemies.

Both tell of God's salvation. Not only that, the preamble to each recording of the Ten Commandments simply identifies who God is in the context of the Egyptian deliverance.

Deuteronomy 5:6 states, "I am the Lord your God, who brought you out of Egypt, out of the land of slavery." The same verse precedes the Ten Commandments in Exodus 20. This story and this first verse should never be separated from the commandments. To divide the story and, in particular, that preamble, is to completely misunderstand the purpose and the meaning of those commandments. I wish that every time we taught young people to memorize the Ten Commandments, or put them up in front of one of our churches, we would include this introduction that tells of God's salvation.

For the Israelite, salvation always preceded the Ten Commandments. The Ten Commandments came to a people who were free. They had been delivered from bondage. They had been delivered from defeat in battles with foreign kings. They had overcome because of that gift of grace, and it was to a free people that the Ten Commandments came. To separate the Ten Commandments from that story is to divorce them from their basis, root, and meaning. In fact, if I were going to translate these verses, I would put a big *therefore* between that first verse and the rest of the commandments. I would have the passage read, "I am the Lord your God, who has brought you out of the land of Egypt, out of the house of bondage. Therefore, you shall have no other gods before me. . . ." *Therefore* is put there to show the connection.

To summarize, law is never the way to salvation. It is always the *fruit* of salvation given to show redeemed people how to live.

CONCLUSION

Our false views of law—as negative, as picky, as a barrier to salvation, as legalistic—are based on our culture and, in particular, a misunderstanding of what the apostle Paul says about not being under law. His statements have been misconstrued to infer that law is inherently bad. Paul himself says the law is just and good (see Romans 7:12). What Paul said must be understood as applying after the Jewish system had been abused for hundreds of years. For Paul, the term *law* represented the entire Jewish system which, in his day, was a problem. God's law itself is good. Systems that have abused it are not.

If the law itself is instruction in the broad sense, and specific commandments are a manual to saved people, we can begin to believe the law is gracious. Believing this takes us farther along the path toward seeing the graciousness of God more fully.

8

God's Gracious Sabbath

All that was said in the previous chapter about God's gracious law can, of course, be applied to the Sabbath as well, for it is a key part of the law. The Sabbath command is an important and unique one. Its length, the fact that a reason is given for keeping it, and the special explanations connected with the Sabbath make it important enough for us to consider this commandment separately.

The Sabbath speaks of God's grace in two major ways. The first one I call "the practical sense." The second is what I choose to term "the symbolic sense."

PRACTICAL MEANING OF THE SABBATH

We live in a day and age in which people look forward to weekends. The majority of people who live in America, Europe, and many other parts of the world consider it their right to have Saturday and Sunday off from work. One does not have to be religious to receive those days off. In fact, they are considered to be secular holidays. In the time of the Israelites, such a practice was nonexistent, particularly for those who were slaves. Can you imagine what Egyptian masters would have said about Israelite slaves who demanded a weekend off? Even if they had said God told them to do it, it would have been impossible to keep the Sabbath in Egypt. The God of slaves would have not been considered important enough to obey or to follow. So the Israelites were used to working seven days a week, year in and year out. God's command to rest on the Seventh day would have been greatly appreciated in a very practical sense by people who worked every day and had no freedom.

We lived for a number of years in close proximity to the Mong people in Thailand. As in many societies, the women worked harder than anybody else. They not only took care of the home chores, like cooking and child care, but they also worked in the fields, moving up and down those mountainous areas, weeding crops, planting, and harvesting. It is backbreaking toil. They knew no day of rest in their native culture, except perhaps feast days and certain yearly festivals such as New Year's. Those people welcomed the news of the Sabbath, particularly the women. Their husbands would tell them to go to work every day, but on the Sabbath day they had a command from God not to work, and that command took priority over their husbands' commands. They loved the Sabbath like Israelite slaves loved the Sabbath.

The Sabbath delivers people, particularly overachievers, from pushing themselves too hard. Many students feel they need to study every day. Other feel the pressures of work and special duties. There are always things they must do at home or at the office. Our society encourages us to be industrious, but some take this too far. The Sabbath is meant to protect those who would attempt to do too much. If you examine the commandment closely, the original statements in Exodus 20 and Deuteronomy 5 say nothing about worship. They simply say to rest on the Sabbath day, to refrain from work, and to avoid engaging in regular activities. This is to be true not only for the heads of households, but for the animals, workers, servants, and slaves that may be connected to a household. It is to be God's rest day for everybody. What a wonderful day! What a gracious gift.

SYMBOLIC MEANING OF THE SABBATH

Not only did the Sabbath give rest in a practical sense to people who were used to working all week, but it also had a deep symbolism in connection with God's grace. This symbolic sense is seen in three major areas of life.

The first area is theological symbolism. The Sabbath points to God's creation and God's salvation. In the two statements of the Ten Commandments, the reason for reverencing the day differs in Exodus 20 and in Deuteronomy 5. Exodus 20 says the Sabbath should be kept as a memorial of the God who created the world, and at the end of that creation, rested on the seventh day (see verses 8-11). So the Sabbath is a sign of creation. Our creation, of course, was an action of grace by God. He didn't have to make us. He brought this world into existence by His own free choice. Our very existence and everything that's beautiful about this world is a gift from God's hand. It's His handiwork. And resting on the Sabbath celebrates our own existence and the pleasantness of that life as a gift from His hands.

In Deuteronomy 5 the reason for keeping the Sabbath is God's great deliverance in the Exodus (verse 15)—the liberation of a slave people from their miserable existence under the Egyptian taskmasters into the freedom of being God's people. The Sabbath, then, symbolized God's salvation by grace. This doesn't mean that one type of symbolism is right and the other wrong. They simply complement each other.

God did not have to choose Israel as His people. He certainly was under no obligation to save them except to keep the promises that He made. But those promises themselves were based upon His grace and His goodness. The Sabbath was the day when the Israelites celebrated their freedom from slavery, and it was only because of this deliverance that they could have a day of rest on which to celebrate it. They could bask in the freedom that God had given them and remember what

God had done in saving them. The weekly repose also gave those who worked for the Israelites the Sabbath Day's rest and a taste of the graciousness of God.

The second thing that the Sabbath symbolizes is the identity of the people of Israel. The Sabbath was to be the sign of who they were. It was to identify them as a separate people. An interesting text in Exodus 31:13 says, "You must observe my Sabbaths. This will be a sign between me and you for the generations to come, so you may know that I am the Lord, who makes you holy." Similar statements also occur in the book of Ezekiel 20:12, 20.

This whole set of passages has often been misunderstood. In some versions the words *holy* or *to make holy* are translated as "sanctify" or "to sanctify." People have said this is a sign that God makes people good or holy. The conclusion is that the Sabbath shows your holiness, or the Sabbath shows that God can make you good or holy. To a certain extent, that's true—at least in the sense that God can cleanse us and give us the strength and the courage to live for Him. However, keeping the Sabbath is not necessarily a sign that a person is holy in a behavioral sense.

Basically, the passage means the Sabbath is a sign that God set Israel apart as a special people for Himself. To be sanctified is to be set apart for a holy purpose or to have God as the One who makes holy. To the Israelites, it didn't mean that they were righteous or better than anyone else, but rather that they were special to God. They were His chosen covenant people, and to keep the Sabbath celebrated who they were (i.e., God's chosen). It was a sign of identity, like the passport that one carries showing what country he is a citizen of. To abandon that passport or to throw it away makes one lose his identity as a person, as a citizen of a particular country, and his ability to travel freely from place to place. The Sabbath was a sign to Israel that she belonged to God. Abandoning the Sabbath would have meant abandoning the sign that she belonged. It would be much like a married couple tearing up the marriage certificate and destroying the evidence of their pledged love—the outward symbol that they belong together. Maybe they'd even go so far as to change their names. It would be an attempt to destroy the symbolism and all the things that bind them together. The Sabbath, then, was a sign of Israel's identity as God's people.

One of the major problems in our world today is that people lack identity—they don't know who they are. People without roots are the ones most tempted to break the laws of God and of man. Those who have no sense of where they came from, where they are going, and whom they belong to are the most likely to suffer psychological and emotional damage. The Sabbath is God's gracious gift of identity that, if celebrated, demonstrates who we are and to whom we belong. Certainly a sign showing that you belong to the King of the universe is a most precious gift.

The third major area of Sabbath symbolism is the role that the Sabbath plays in the restoration that God foretells for Israel.

The greatest prophets of Israel—Isaiah, Jeremiah, and Ezekiel—all mention the Sabbath as a facet of the restoration God brings to His people. In fact, in Jeremiah 17, keeping the Sabbath is part of the path to God's offered restoration. In Isaiah 66:23, the prophet declares that in the new heavens and the new earth, keeping the Sabbath will still be important. And in the renewed and restored Israel, described in Ezekiel, chapters 44-46, the Sabbath figures prominently as a day that is to be kept, remembered, and reverenced.

So the Sabbath, then, is a symbol of God as Creator and His grace in making us; of God as redeemer and His grace in saving us. Because we are believers in Christ and thus comprise "spiritual Israel," we, along with ancient Israel, are the children of promise. Therefore, the Sabbath remains the symbol of our special relationship with the gracious God who gives us our identity, peoplehood, and knowledge of who we are.

The Sabbath is also part of God's plan of restoration. It speaks not only of what He has been in the past, but also of what He intends to be in the future. Thus, the Sabbath, in both the practical and symbolic sense, is a statement of God's grace to people that is to be cherished and rejoiced in.

A STORY OF GRACE

Rosa Parks started a revolution just by sitting. She was tired and wanted to rest. She headed home after finishing work at a tailor's shop. Her feet hurt. She couldn't face the thought of having to stand up all the way home, so Rosa refused the bus driver's order to give up her seat so a white man could sit down. Two policemen came and took Parks down to the police station, where officials booked her for violation of the city bus ordinance. At Rosa's trial the judge found her guilty. He fined her $14.00, including court costs, but Rosa had already sparked a revolution. Outraged blacks boycotted the bus system. Their leaders chose Martin Luther King, Jr., as president of the Montgomery Improvement Association, and the legalized segregation of blacks and whites was halted. Rosa's rest symbolized the revolution. Her sitting down demonstrated how tired her people were of the situation in Montgomery, Alabama, in 1955. Who would have believed that something so simple as resting could be such a powerful symbol and revolutionary spark?

Our world needs a new revolution. Many of us are tired—not just our feet, but our whole beings. In the hustle and bustle and rush of life, we have too much to do in too little time, and we're tired.

Rosa's rest changed the whole course of history for her people. God's proclamation of the Sabbath rest proclaimed a revolution for His people, Israel, who were slaves to the Egyptians, even as the blacks had been slaves to an unjust system.

Resting is a revolutionary statement of grace, which says: I don't have to earn my way to salvation. I don't have to work. God's grace tells me that I can rest in His love and acceptance, and that I don't have to do anything to merit it. I can be a child of His, and I can symbolize my belonging to Him by resting.

The Sabbath is a powerful statement of God's grace. Our identity, our past, and our future are in His hands. We should allow no man or society or culture to enslave us, for those who rest on Sabbath symbolize their freedom in God and their relationship to Him.

9

God's Gracious Covenant

Some words carry with them so much extra baggage that they might be better disposed of or replaced. At times I suspect the word *covenant* fits in that category. Say the word, and people visualize long theological arguments and lengthy lists of things differentiating old and new covenants. They hear people talking heatedly about works and faith. For many, *covenant* is a word only theologians should wrestle with. I want to put aside the debate and complicated arguments and simply try to demonstrate how the covenant is like everything else we've studied this far—a gracious gift of God.

THE MEANING OF *COVENANT*

Covenant is an important word in the Old Testament. It occurs 287 times and figures prominently at crucial points in divine history. The covenant is so important to Christians that we named the Bible after it! The word *testament* is simply an older, English word meaning "covenant." Calling the two major sections of our Bible *Old* and *New Testament* demonstrates how widely Christians have used the term. Some, in fact, see the term as representing the major theological concept uniting these two sections of God's Word.

Numerous synonyms for *covenant* exist. Some suggest "contract," "bond," "alliance," "agreement," or "treaty." We do know that the way the Old Testament describes covenants closely resembles examples of ancient treaties we have from the Hittite people. Some of these synonyms would work well in describing the Old Testament covenants that were made between two human parties. The kind of covenant, however, that most interests us are those made between God and human beings. In this case the best synonym is *relationships.* A covenant is a defined relationship between God and His people.

In the Old Testament there seem to have been three major kinds of covenants. The first was a parity covenant. This was an agreement between equals and was entered into for the benefit of both parties. Divine-human covenants are not generally described in this way.

The other two types of covenants were the royal grant covenant and the ruler-vassal covenant. There are the covenants that in certain ways parallel the God-human relationships described in the Old Testament. Four major characteristics of these divine-human relationships powerfully illustrate God's grace.

GOD INITIATES HIS COVENANTS/RELATIONSHIPS

All major Old Testament covenants were God initiated. Man does not go to God and ask for a relationship. Man, in fact, has no basis on which to ask for an agreement with God. God always starts the process. God was the initiator in all five major Old Testament covenants. Those covenants were with Noah, Abraham, Moses, and David, and the new covenant described in Jeremiah 31.

The statement that makes this clear is, "I will establish my covenant with you." God is the divine "I," and humans are always the "you." This terminology occurs in Genesis 6:18; 9:9ff;

17:7; Exodus 6:4; 34:10, 27; Deuteronomy 29:12, 14; Isaiah 55:3; Jeremiah 31:31-33; 32:40; Ezekiel 16:60; Haggai 2:5, and it rings like a resounding chorus throughout the Old Testament. God reaches out to establish a relationship with humankind. They can't do it, but He graciously can and does.

I can't invite myself into a personal friendship with the President of the United States. I doubt I could get even a brief appointment with the man. He would have to do the initiating. This is even more so when it comes to our Heavenly Father. I can't ask for a relationship with God—He must start the process. The fact that He has is a statement of His grace.

THE COVENANT IS A GOOD DEAL

I can hear you now. Some are saying, "Yes, God initiated the whole thing, but it's a good deal for Him, not for us!" In response I simply ask you to listen to the benefits that come from the covenant—the gracious promises God makes to those with whom He initiates a relationship.

To Noah, God promised never to destroy the earth with a flood again (see Genesis 9:11). To Abraham, God pledged the land of Canaan, a great nation as his posterity, and blessings of all kinds. Moses received the renewal of earlier promises and the pledge of deliverance from Egyptian slavery. David was promised a lasting dynasty and rest in the Promised Land. The new covenant in Jeremiah 31 pledged that God would write His laws on our hearts, that all would know Him, and that they would be His people (verses 33, 34). He also promised to forgive their sins.

These are *good* promises. What God says He will do for His people is attractive. God doesn't initiate relationships solely for His benefit. They are to help people. They are a good idea. In other words, God comes bearing gracious promises of good gifts and a close relationship with Him.

THE COVENANT AND ITS PROMISES ARE UNDESERVED

The amazing thing is that these God-initiated, good-promise relationships are totally undeserved. They are not earned but given in love and mercy to those who need them and whose need is the only real criteria for receiving them.

In some ways, Noah seems to be an exception to this rule. Noah is said to have been a righteous man (see Genesis 6:9 and 7:1), and perhaps this covenant was made just because he was good. It should be noted, however, that the passage also says in Genesis 6:8 that Noah found grace (favor) in God's eyes. It should also be remembered that Noah was by no means perfect (see Genesis 9:20ff), and that the basic promises of the covenant given to him pertained to *others*. The good promise of the Noachian covenant was that the posterity of Noah and the animals would not be slain in another flood. This good gift to the human race and animal kingdom certainly was not based on their good deeds.

Abraham was far from perfect. No statements of his works of righteousness precede God's promises to him. In fact, Genesis specifically says that his righteousness came from his belief in God's promises (see Genesis 15:6). His righteousness, then, was based not on what he did prior to the promises, but on his acceptance of the undeserved promises! *Righteousness is faith in God's grace.*

The sins of David, Moses, and Israel are well known. God's promises to Israel and David's posterity were magnanimous gifts of grace, based not on merit but on God's goodness.

The new covenant promises of Jeremiah 31 are even more amazing. God's people Israel were deep in sin. The Babylonian captivity had already taken place for some, and the handwriting was on the wall. Jerusalem and the precious temple were soon to be destroyed. This judgment of God was deserved because of Israel's persistent rebellion. In the midst of all this, however, came the promise of a new relationship with Israel. The old relationship was destroyed, not by God, but by the people themselves (see Jeremiah 31:32). The new covenant was, as usual, initiated by God, and its promises were even better than the old promises.

The people destroyed the old relationship by their sin. God not only forgave but also promised a new relationship that was even better than the old one. God did all that even *before* the change of behavior took place on the people's part. This was undeserved grace.

We humans are not used to operating that way. When children sin, we take away privileges—not add them. Criminals are put on probation, and their freedom is restricted. Flunking a test means the student must work even harder to make the grade. But here God does the opposite. To the sinner who has divorced Him, He promises a new marriage with even greater privileges and more intimacy. What a God and what grace!

GOD BEARS LONG WITH COVENANT BREAKERS

The last factor about these God-human relationship covenants is that God bears long—graciously long—with those who break them. He goes far beyond normal expectations of patience. He doesn't file for divorce—the people always do. That always comes after they've long abused the undeserved privilege God has given them.

By the time of Jeremiah, God had already covenanted with Israel for over 1,000 years, counting from the time of Abraham. After all that time, Jeremiah 31 promises a new relationship. One might excuse God if the new relationship had been made with a new group of people. That, of course, was not the case. He simply reestablished a new relationship based on even better terms with the old group of people. The Lord says, "Only if the heavens above can be measured and the foundations of the earth below be searched out will I reject all the descendants of Israel because of all they have done" (Jeremiah 31:37).

The enduring patience of God in maintaining this relationship is based on His gracious, undying love.

A STORY OF GRACE

In a moment of temporary insanity, we bought the house for a small amount down. Our parents had given us some money to help finance our children's education. We had heard real estate was a great investment. We decided to invest that money in the somewhat rundown dwelling. Before we knew what had happened, the paperwork was done, and the house was ours—rather, our obligation.

It didn't take long to realize we had been foolish. Time, money, or both were needed when things broke down. Tenants are not always honest. Those who are honest are not always employed. Those who are honest and employed often move. The rent payments that were supposed to cover mortgage payments were often not there. We found it hard to evict nonpayers. The list of woes is well known to any who "own" such property.

We were stuck. Legally, we were supposed to pay off. Property values fell in our area, and the house deteriorated. We found ourselves in an unpleasant situation.

In that crisis we experienced a moment of grace. The contract was held by the former owner. He saw our predicament and offered to discount the house heavily. Legally, he was required to do nothing. He had every right to demand full payment, but instead, he, on his own initiative—in an undeserved act—reduced the amount of money we owed. It was, in essence, a gift.

The owner had offered a covenant. We had accepted but had trouble keeping our part of the bargain. The owner, though under no obligation to do so, made a new agreement with us that we could handle. The God of the Old Testament covenant is even more gracious.

10

People Gifted—Prophets, Kings, and Judges

Undoubtedly my title will be misunderstood. Most will think it is a mistake and should read "Gifted People" rather than "People Gifted." The title is correct. Prophets, kings, and judges were not so much people who possessed special abilities and gifts, as they were ordinary people whom God had given as gracious gifts to help His people. God endowed them with special talents needed for their work, but these talents were God's gifts so that His people might have their needs supplied. These special offices that God ordained were therefore institutions of grace.

PROPHETS

The prophet was specially called and fitted by God as His spokesman. While priests were man's representatives to God, the prophet was God's representative to mankind. The priest's role was hereditary, but the prophet's role came only by divine call. The prophet taught righteousness, spirituality, and ethics.

Prophets called God's people back to relationship with Him. How, then, was their work a statement of grace?

First, prophets usually came at a time of crisis. Often a crisis was brought on by the sins of the people. Jeremiah and Ezekiel are excellent examples of this.

Jeremiah declared God's word for forty years during the difficult times leading up to Judah's exile in Babylon. He clearly pointed to the sin that caused Israel's downfall and called the people back to God.

Ezekiel followed up the ministry of Jeremiah. He functioned in Babylon among the people who had just gone into exile. He shattered their false hopes of an early return to Jerusalem and told them how they must live in light of the momentous events then taking place.

Many have never sensed the implications of the fact, that God had sent these prophets at the very time when Israel did *not* deserve God's help. *In spite* of Israel's sin, God graciously sent prophets to show Israel the way back to Him and promised restoration. This is grace.

For the Israelites, then, the prophetic *gift* was just that—a desired gift of God. When Eldad and Medad prophesied in the Israelite camp, Aaron thought to stop them, but Moses said, "I wish that all the Lord's people were prophets and that the Lord would put his Spirit on them" (Numbers 11:29).

Through the prophet, God warned His people to turn from sin (see 2 Kings 17:13, 23). This was help for them. The prophet also could arise in answer to prayer to instruct God's people so that they could escape harm. This was the case in 2 Chronicles 20 when God spoke through Jahaziel. This message from God led the king and people to worship and praise God (see 2 Chronicles 20:14-19). The next day, this prophecy resulted in Israel's deliverance from their enemies.

As part of God's future plans for the restoration of His people, the prophetic gift played a part. Joel prophesied of a day when God would pour out His Spirit, and Israel's sons and daughters would prophesy (see Joel 2:28, 29). Malachi 4:5, 6 says that before the great and terrible day of the Lord, Yahweh will send the prophet Elijah to bring families back together. Prophets and prophecy are part of what God gives to restore and bless His people.

KINGS

Most Israelite kings were not what they were supposed to be. Often they led their people into sin. In fact, the very desire for a king in the beginning is portrayed as something undesirable. The people's desire for a king evidenced their rejection of God's rule over them in favor of being like the nations around them (see 1 Samuel 8). If this was the case, how could kingship be seen as a gift of God's grace?

In the midst of many weak and sinful kings, one king was quite successful—David. His dynasty lasted over 400 years, and he was regarded as the ideal king. He unified the country and established Jerusalem. He laid the groundwork for the subsequent building of the temple at the capital.

Although David was less than perfect and most of his successors even less so, God provided much instruction for Israel as to what an ideal king should be like. The prophets went even further and prophesied of the day when there really would come a true king sent by God. This king of David's line would finally do all that godly kings should.

One of the most moving passages about this ideal king is recorded in Isaiah 11:1-10. Note what this special king is like. God's Spirit will be on him, and his delight will be serving God. He will rule in righteousness and justice, while especially caring for the poor and meek. He will destroy evil. Hurt and destruction will cease, and peace and tranquility will come over the earth. Doesn't that sound good?

In fact, most of the passages that Christians see as prophesies of Jesus in the Old Testament are directly related to this ideal king of David's line for which all Israel was hoping and praying. God took this kingship institution that was much abused and molded it into a vehicle for His promises of hope for the future. Certainly the arrival of such a king is the supreme gift of grace. Certainly looking at the rule of various leaders today can make us long for God's kingship and kingdom and rejoice in His promises of the *real* King.

JUDGES

The word *judge* conjures up in most minds the picture of a solemn, robed dignitary who decides your guilt or innocence in a court of law. The Old Testament judge hardly fit that image. While he or she did dispense justice, that justice was seen more as vindication for God's people than as punishment for the guilty. The word *judges* in the Old Testament book of Judges would probably better be translated as *saviors*. These saviors were charismatically empowered by God's Spirit to deliver Israel from oppression and preserve the nation. The gracious gift of these deliverers is best understood by a closer look at the book of Judges.

The main body of the book of Judges goes through six cycles. During these six cycles, there were twelve judges. Each of these cycles followed the same pattern, which is outlined in Judges 2, 11, and 23, and illustrated in each of the six cycles. It goes like this: (1) Israel did evil and served Baal; (2) the Lord gave them over to plunderers over whom they could not win victories; (3) the people cried out to God; (4) God raised up a judge to deliver them; (5) the people served God while the judge was alive and the land rested; and (6) when the judge died, Israel went back to sin—even worse sin than before.

From the standpoint of grace, several things need to be emphasized in the cycle. God sent these deliverers, not because the people deserved it, but because the people asked out of great need. They were in the midst of suffering because of sin. The deliverer came to save, and the saving led to a following of God. The actual coming of the deliverer was then an "unmerited favor."

God kept this up over a long period. Over and over again, He saved Israel, even when each fall became progressively worse. The patient grace of God in saving over and over again is amazing. The stories of deliverance are told in such a way that there is no doubt as to the source of deliverance—Israel's gracious God.

CONCLUSION

More could be said, but it should be clear by now that

priests, prophets, kings, and judges were God's gracious gifts to His people. They were to help and deliver.

One office that I've chosen not to discuss in detail but that deserves further study is that of the wise man—the giver of proverbs and the explainer of life's anomalies. Certainly the books of Proverbs and Job, which came from such wise men, are also gifts of grace to help us live more happy day-to-day lives. They make us better able to grapple with the challenges that face us. In every situation God, in His mercy, sends the person needed for the benefit of His people. That is grace.

A STORY OF GRACE

A common dream people have is to be in some kind of trouble and feel the desperate need to cry out for help or warning and find themselves dumb. Repeated attempts to scream bring no result, and only deeper frustration. That dream came true for me when I wound up in Tokyo in the middle of the night without a translator.

The whole episode began with my forgetting our plane tickets on the dresser of our Honolulu lodgings. No ticket, no travel. A hasty dash to retrieve the tickets and speed back to the airport was not quite quick enough. We missed our plane and had to wait for what seemed forever for the next one.

We had no way to contact those who were to meet us in Tokyo. Besides that, the delay made our arrival take place in the middle of the night. In 1968, the night crew in Tokyo didn't seem to speak English. I don't know how many people I tried. They were all friendly, but we couldn't communicate. Talking slowly didn't help. Besides that, how many in Tokyo know about Seventh-day Adventists? We had about decided that we would spend what was left of the night in the airport and try to find someone who understood and could help in the morning. Then she appeared. It wouldn't have taken much to have us believe she had dropped from heaven! She was our prophet delivering messages we would otherwise not have been able to hear, and our judge, graciously delivering us from a bad situation that was of *my* making. Soon, needed connections were made, and we escaped from the airport. God's gracious giving of messengers is just like that!

IV

Grace in Texts and Words

The first two major sections of this book deal with what I call the "macrostructure" of the Old Testament. They are the larger view—the forest rather than the trees. I believe we need to begin here in seeing grace in the Old Testament because it shows us that the concept comprises the very bones and framework of the book. We must go on, however.

It is not wrong to look at the "*micro*structure," or trees, in the forest of the Old Testament. We cannot forget that the concept of grace is in the smaller structure as well as the larger one. In this section, then, we attempt to examine grace in individual texts and words in the Old Testament itself and even how some of these have been used in the New Testament.

11

The Old Testament's Most Used Text

When someone important gives a clear statement of who he is and what he stands for, people listen. That should be particularly true if God is the one making the declaration. This statement becomes crucial when it is repeated over and over again like the theme of a symphony. More than that, this statement should be loved and cherished if it is a statement of God's grace and love. All the above are true in relation to the passage we will consider in this chapter. This passage is the most repeated verse in the Old Testament.

GOD REVEALS HIMSELF

Israel had just danced in idolatrous worship before the golden calf, and it seemed for a while that they would be destroyed (see Exodus 32). God relented on the destruction and said He would help get them into Canaan as He promised, but He wouldn't go before them—He would send His angel.

Moses went to the tent of meeting to speak with God. Moses told how he had been asked to lead the people and had been told his name was known by God and that he had found favor before Him. Moses, however, felt the need to really experience God's presence and to have that presence as he led the people into Canaan. If Israel were God's people, how could they and others know Him if He weren't with them? Moses directly asked to see God's glorious presence (see Exodus 33:18). God promised to cause His goodness to pass in front of Moses. When that happened, God issued the basic statement of who He was:

> He passed in front of Moses, proclaiming, "The Lord, the Lord, the compassionate and gracious God, slow to anger, abounding in love and faithfulness, maintaining love to thousands, and forgiving wickedness, rebellion and sin. Yet he does not leave the guilty unpunished; he punishes the children and their children for the sin of the fathers to the third and fourth generation (Exodus 34:6, 7).

Moses responded by bowing to the ground and worshiping. When God is seen for what He is, humans can only worship. Moses then proceeded to ask God to live up to His name and forgive Israel. God proceeded to do just that!

Several things should be noticed about this passage in Exodus 34:6, 7, which Jewish scholars call "the thirteen attributes." First, notice how these attributes are balanced. The tremendous love and grace and mercy are balanced by righteousness, justice, and holiness. God's mercy, love, and grace would be meaningless to us unless He was also holy and just. To protect the child of God, sin and the guilty must, in the end, be dealt with so salvation and judgment can both occur.

Second, the extent of God's grace far surpasses the extent of His punishment. Punishment extends to three or four generations, but the love and grace goes to thousands of generations.

Most traditional English Bible versions mistranslate this passage and the similar passages in Exodus 20:5, 6 and Deuteronomy 5:9, 10—the second of the Ten Commandments.

In all of these passages, the Hebrew word for *generation* is missing. The translators supply the word *generations* in the part of the passages dealing with sin and leave it out in the part of the verses talking of God's mercy. Thus, most people understand that God's mercy extends to thousands of people and His judgment on sin to three and four generations. The word *generation* should be supplied to *both* parts of the verse. God's mercy extends to thousands of *generations*, while the punishment for sin to only three or four generations. This interpretation is further supported by similar passages in 1 Chronicles 16:15 and Psalm 105:8, which actually include the word *generations* in the Hebrew text.

This powerful statement about the enduring mercy of God came right after Israel had sinned grievously and in no way deserved mercy. This revelation of God came in response to Moses' plea on behalf of the people. The revelation of mercy to the undeserving was followed by merciful action and a renewal of the covenant.

REPETITION OF THIS TEXT

This classic description of God is recalled repeatedly in the rest of the Old Testament—more than any other passage. Major repetitions with similar wording include Numbers 14:18; Nehemiah 9:17; Psalm 86:15; 103:8; 145:8; Jeremiah 32:18; Joel 2:13; Jonah 4:2; and Nahum 1:3. In most cases, the passages form either the basis of an appeal for God's forgiveness or an explanation of why God was gracious to His people.

The use of these verses in Jonah is an especially interesting one. Jonah had just prophesied in no uncertain terms that in forty days Nineveh would be destroyed. In response to this prophetic proclamation, Nineveh repents. When God saw this repentance, He repented! He had compassion and did not destroy. Jonah became very angry because his status as a prophet was in jeopardy. People would think his prediction was false. Jonah told God that this was the reason he didn't want to come prophesy to Nineveh in the first place! He knew that God was merciful and gracious, slow to anger, and full of love. Jonah knew God would be merciful, and he didn't want to be made a fool of. He had no desire for Nineveh—Israel's enemy—to escape, but knew God did. Sure enough—just as he had thought—God turned out to be gracious and merciful—even to foreign nations. God had great love even for the enemies of His people and forgave them just as He had forgiven Israel over and over again.

God is gracious, and that grace is universal. That grace is *more* important than the literal fulfilling of a time prophecy and the reputation of God's messenger.

If the many repetitions of this verse mean anything, it says that Israel saw the characteristics of God as mentioned in this verse as the most central and basic truths one could know about God. Israel understood her God, Yahweh, in His essential being as merciful, gracious, forgiving, and just. For the Old Testament as well as the New, God is love. God is grace. God is faithfulness. God is forgiveness. He is all of these things to people who don't deserve them; and He is all of these things repeatedly. He is slow, very slow, to anger.

A STORY OF GRACE

I met Lucy when I got on the bus heading out of Los Angeles. It was Easter weekend, and the bus was crowded. After waiting in line for what seemed like ages, I got one of the last vacant seats—next to Lucy.

As we headed north into the night, she began to talk. She told me of her work as a salesperson in an elite department store and of the men in her life. The longer she talked, the more nervous I became. I knew when she found out who I was, she'd be embarrassed, but I just listened helplessly.

Finally, she asked, "What do you do?"

I tried to delay the agony by replying, "I teach."

"What?" she said.

"Guess," I returned.

When it finally came out that I was a minister, she explained, "I've never sat this close to a priest before!"

Immediately she began to back up from some of her earlier tales. "I really didn't party that much," she said, "and really didn't behave that loosely with men," she continued.

"Wait," I said. "Don't worry about all that. God meets people right where they are." She suddenly became strangely quiet and listened as I tried to tell her about the love of God as best I could and the Jesus who forgives sinners.

Things went well until I said, "God is like a father."

"I hope not," she said. "My dad never cared for me." It was like opening up an infected, festering wound. Out tumbled a lifelong story of not being cared about—first, because she was darker than her siblings; second, because she seemed to do everything wrong. Coming home to visit from her job in Los Vegas, she had had an auto accident. She called home and asked for help. Her father had said, "You're a big girl now, Lucy; take care of yourself!" Even now, her parents hardly spoke to her. When she saw parents and children come into her place of work and show love, her heart longed to be loved as a daughter. Finally, she asked me, "If I were your daughter, would you like me?"

I got a huge lump in my throat as I mumbled, "Yes."

Lucy couldn't understand God's grace because she had never seen it in anyone in her life. Has the God who is merciful and gracious broken through to us? Have we been His emissaries of forgiving grace to others? Israel saw that grace after the golden calf. Have you experienced it in your life? The Lucys of the world need to hear it. Like God's repetition of His grace to Israel, they need to hear it over and over and over again.

12

Other Texts of Grace

Besides the most-repeated text on grace in the Old Testament that we discussed in the previous chapter, many other individual texts also tell of grace. Those discussed are only samples of what can be found and are by no means exhaustive. The format followed is simple: I give the text and either quote or summarize it, and then give a brief explanation. Take some time to let these statements of grace sink into your *heart* as well as your head.

GENESIS 15:6

> Abraham believed the Lord, and he credited it to him as righteousness.

In Genesis 15, God had just renewed His promise to Abraham that he would have a son and become the father of a numberless multitude. Abraham was credited with righteousness for believing that fantastic promise. He had done no great deed to deserve the promise. The promise didn't hinge on his obedience. It was just a great promise. Abraham was considered righteous because he believed it.

One even wonders about the strength and durability of Abraham's faith. In the very next chapter, he took Hagar as a wife to try to "help" Yahweh produce a son. In the chapter after that (see Genesis 17:18), Abraham asked that the son of his union with Hagar might be accepted by God. All this makes the faith of Genesis 15:6 sound a bit shaky. In the gracious eyes of Yahweh it was evidently enough to have Abraham declared righteous. I call this "righteous by very shaky faith."

2 SAMUEL 7:13-15

> I will establish the throne of his kingdom forever. I will be his father, and he will be my son. When he does wrong, I will punish him with the rod of men. . . . But my love will never be taken away from him, as I took it away from Saul. . . . Your house and your kingdom will endure forever before me.

This was God's promise to David concerning his son Solomon. What is interesting is that Solomon was not born yet, and David's life with all its sin lay before him. The promise included leading a wayward son back to him after he sinned. In other words, the promise assumed the sin and unworthiness of the promised receiver. In spite of that, the promise was given. Love, guidance, and an enduring kingdom were promised to the undeserving.

ISAIAH 40-66

This whole section is filled with gracious promises showing the unfailing mercy, love, and forgiveness of God to His people. True, they had sinned and gone astray, but He promised to bring them back again, so they had nothing to fear. Those who wonder if God cares would do well to read this section of Scripture over and over again.

A kind of summary sample is Isaiah 63:7-9:

> I will tell of the kindnesses of the Lord, the deeds for which he is to be praised, according to all the Lord has done for us—yes, the many good things he has done for the house of Israel, according to his compassion and many kindnesses. He said, "surely they are my people, sons who will not be false to me"; and so he became their Savior. In all their distress he too was distressed, and the angel of his presence saved them. In his love and mercy he redeemed them; he lifted them up and carried them all the days of old.

Even though the Israelites sinned, God would save them again in their distress. He would blot out their sins and remember their transgressions no more (see Isaiah 43:25). He would care for the poor, the brokenhearted, and the prisoners (see Isaiah 61:1). He would create new heavens and a new earth (see Isaiah 66:22). All needs would be cared for by a gracious God.

JEREMIAH 31:31-34

In Jeremiah 31:3, 4, the Lord declares,

> I have loved you with an everlasting love; therefore I have continued my faithfulness to you. Again I will build you, and you shall be built, O virgin Israel! Again you shall adorn yourself with timbrels, and shall go forth in the dance of the merrymakers (RSV).

Later in the same chapter, Jeremiah spells out how this love and building God has promised will take place. It comes through a new covenant, or relationship, that God Himself makes and fashions.

> I will make a new covenant with the house of Israel and the house of Judah, not like the covenant which I made with their fathers when I took them by the hand to bring them out of the land of Egypt, my covenant which they broke, though I was their husband, says the Lord. But this is the covenant which I will make with the house of Israel after those days, says the Lord: I will put my law within them, and I will write it upon their hearts; and I will be their God,

> and they shall be my people. . . . I will forgive their iniquity, and I will remember their sin no more (Jeremiah 31:31-34, RSV).

God promised to do all this while Israel was still far from Him and about to make her divorce from Him final! God saw a future renewal of relationship—or covenant—and marriage, and it was to be done *by* Him, in spite of the people. Notice the constant repetition of "I" in the passage. God as the speaker says, "I will make," "I will put," "I will be," "I will forgive," etc. It is His work—a work of grace.

One should also note that these promises are better than the former ones. The new covenant is even better than the older one because the people broke the old one. God Himself will change hearts in this new covenant and will forgive the past wrongs. That's gracious news!

EZEKIEL 36:24—38

This entire passage should be read carefully, but for space reasons, I quote its central essence:

> I will gather you from all the countries and bring you back into your own land. I will sprinkle clean water on you, and you will be clean; I will cleanse you from all your impurities and from all your idols. I will give you a new heart and put a new spirit in you; I will remove from you your heart of stone and give you a heart of flesh. And I will put my Spirit in you and move you to follow my decrees and be careful to keep my laws. . . .
>
> Then you will remember your evil ways and wicked deeds, and you will loathe yourselves for your sins (Ezekiel 36:24-27, 31).

Again we find ourselves in the context of the exile, with Israel still in a state of sin. Again we see the "I," "I," "I" repetition in which God is the initiator of all these gracious acts on behalf of His people. This passage reveals the sequence of all this in a unique way. One would normally expect repentance to be a condition for these promised blessings. Some probably assume that in the earlier verses, the people of God had already mourned for their sin and in penitence come to God. He had then made these gracious promises. In some cases, that sequence is present. In this situation, however, it is not.

What Ezekiel saw was a tremendous outpouring of grace to an undeserving people, which *led them to repentance.* In Ezekiel's mind, repentance and loathing for sin were produced from the generous, free stream of salvation and blessings.

The reason for this is clear. A spiritually dead Israel couldn't do anything; only God could. Ezekiel's vision of the valley of dry bones demonstrated this vividly, in the very next chapter (37).

Israel is pictured as a pile of very dead, dry bones in the middle of a valley. Dead bones can't do anything. On that pile of dead bones, the Spirit of God moves in power, bringing them to life and turning them into a vast army. Can dead bones live? By themselves, no way. By the gracious, sovereign power of the Lord, absolutely!

HOSEA 11:1-11

Listen to Hosea's moving description of God's feelings for Israel:

> When Israel was a child, I loved him, and out of Egypt I called my son. But the more I called Israel, the further they went from me. They sacrificed to the Baals and they burned incense to images. It was I who taught Ephraim to walk, taking them by the arms; but they did not realize it was I who healed them. I led them with cords of human kindness, with ties of love; I lifted the yoke from their neck and bent down to feed them. . . .
>
> How can I give you up, Ephraim? How can I hand you over, Israel? . . . My heart is changed within me; all my compassion is aroused. I will not carry out my fierce anger, nor devastate Ephraim again. For I am God, and not man—the Holy One among you. I will not come in wrath (Hosea 11:1-4, 8, 9).

The sin of the northern kingdom of Israel is the setting of

this passage. While God is deeply concerned over their sin, this passage reveals where the *heart* of God is. Many other passages describe what God does in grace and mercy, but Hosea reveals how God *felt* about Israel. God's emotions and pathos are spelled out. God cared deeply about Israel—His compassion was aroused. He could not calmly and coolly respond and carry out the just sentence. Deep in the heart of God, He remembered His child Israel. He remembered teaching her to walk. He had to be gracious.

Hosea reminds us that, in the Old Testament, God's grace is not simply a principle upon which He operates, like gravity is a principle of the cosmos. God's grace is born and operates out of love and compassion—emotions that are felt and experienced. Such statements are enough to drive philosophers crazy, but they bring rejoicing to wayward children who thrive in the warmth of that love.

A STORY OF GRACE

People often remember the small acts of kindness and grace better than the larger, more prominent ones. Perhaps it is because the larger things are expected and don't represent the same kind of thought and emotion the little ones do. It is often the little, unnecessary things that say I really *care*—my heart is involved, and I'm not just doing my duty.

Kathy, my wife, remembers as a girl forgetting small things at home that she wanted to take to school. They weren't necessary—just nice. Reluctantly, she would call her father, who was busy at his job, but how her heart was warmed when he would cheerfully volunteer to take time out and bring them to her, with no scolding or sermons about remembering. Those gracious deliveries made over thirty years ago still bring a warm glow to Kathy when she thinks of them today. They said, "Dad really cared."

When I was a freshman in academy, I wanted a car to tinker with. I didn't have much money—about $50, as I recall. Even in the late 1950s, that wasn't much of a car. I didn't have a driver's license yet, so my dad had to drive me around to various car lots. When you have such a small sum, the money must be spent carefully. For weeks, I scanned ads, made calls, and plotted to visit all the budget used-car places. The process of looking took time. Evening after evening, my busy physician father took me on my rounds. You can guess the kinds of places we went. The best we looked at were on the back row of the cheapest used-car lot on the wrong side of the tracks. I don't remember him ever complaining. Neither do I remember him laughing at me. He let me take my time with that momentous decision. When my "new," ugly, green Chevy sat at the back of the house for months, I wasn't hassled either. As I look back now thirty years later, I smile in amusement at the dreams of youth, but mostly it's a warm smile that recognizes the gracious patience of my father. I bask in the knowledge that he really cared. That kind of love gives a small example of how warming the gracious, undeserved grace of God can be.

13

Grace-filled Words

On the whole, the Old Testament proclaims God's mercy by use of story, symbol, ritual, and act. Whether by story or ritual, however, certain key words are used in these descriptions of grace. A study of these words can teach us more about grace and provide new insight on familiar passages. This chapter examines three key words that can broaden our concept of grace. While there are other words we could study and benefit from, these three are, in my estimation, the most important.

CHESED—COVENANT LOVE

This word, which occurs 243 times in the Old Testament, is translated by eleven different words in the King James Version. The main ones are *mercy* (149), *kindness* (38), and *loving kindness* (30). It has always been difficult for translators to know how to render this word in English. The Revised Standard Version normally uses *steadfast love*. The New International Version uses different words—often even in the same book. For example, in the NIV, Hosea 6:4 renders it *love*, 6:6 translates it *mercy*, and 10:12 uses *unfailing love*.

Most students of the word *chesed* agree that it is often related to the covenant God made with Israel. Thus, my Hebrew teacher taught us to translate it as *covenant loyalty*. It also seems plain that a strong component in the word's meaning is *faithfulness*. The word implies a love and mercy that lasts and is loyal.

While the word can be used of both God and man, it is primarily used to describe the God of Israel who is lovingly faithful to His people. The marvelous thing about the *chesed* of God is what it leads Him to do. It is seen as a basis for a myriad of good things He does for Israel.

It is the way He leads Israel in Exodus 15:13. It is the basis for pardoning sin in Numbers 14:19. It is the source of promise to David's dynasty in 2 Samuel 7:15. It is the reason for Ezra's favorable meeting with Artaxerxes in Ezra 7:28. It makes it possible to enter the temple and worship in Psalm 5:7. It makes the king unmovable in Psalm 21:7. It is the root of help and deliverance in Psalm 44:26. It brings salvation to believers and shame to persecutors in Psalm 57:3. It is the same as granting salvation in Psalm 85:7. It is the source of victory in Psalm 98:2, 3.

The list could go on and on. God's *chesed* is the source of countless merciful and gracious acts that He performs for His people. The most blessed thing of all is that this *chesed* endures forever. It never ceases but lasts on and on. This phraseology is very common, but its most outstanding use is in Psalm 136. There, in the RSV, the continuous refrain, "For his steadfast love endures forever," occurs twenty-six times—once in each verse. What a comfort for God's people is this gracious *chesed*, which knows *no* end.

CHEN—GRACIOUS

The Hebrew word that is actually translated as *grace* in the King James Version Bible is *chen*. It occurs sixty-eight times and is translated as *grace* thirty-eight times and as *favor* twenty-eight times. Most modern versions use these same words to convey its meaning. *Chen* is different from *chesed* in that it is one way. Mankind can show *chesed* to God, but man cannot show *chen* to God. *Chen* is the one-way kindness, grace, or favor that a superior shows to an inferior. People can show *chen* to other people but never to God, for none are superior to Him. Grace as *chen* is the free bestowal of kindness on one who has no claim on the kindness or adequate compensation to make for it.

While humans can show grace by specific deeds, the adjective form of this word, *channun*, or *gracious*, is used *only of God* in the Old Testament. Humans can show sporadic, temporary acts of grace, but only God is, by very essence or nature, truly gracious at all times.

Because God *is* gracious, He does all kinds of gracious things.

> He hears the one who has no mantle to keep warm at night (see Exodus 22:27).
>
> He responds to those sinners who return to him (see 2 Chronicles 30:9).
>
> He does not forsake His sinful people or make an end to them (see Nehemiah 9:17, 31).
>
> He shows love to those who call on Him (see Psalm 86:5).
>
> He provides food for those who fear Him (see Psalm 111:4, 5).
>
> He preserves the simple and saves those brought low (see Psalm 116:5, 6).
>
> He is good to all His creation (see Psalm 145:8, 9).

These acts and others testify of the God who is gracious by his very nature. They demonstrate what He is really like inside and provide hope, comfort, and deliverance to His people.

TSEDEQAH—GRACIOUS

Righteousness is one translation of the important Hebrew root based on the consonants *sdq*. This root occurs over 500 times in the Old Testament. Words based on this root have been translated many different ways, but the nouns are usually rendered something like *righteousness*, *justice*, *vindication*, or some synonym resembling these three words in meaning.

In the Old Testament, *righteousness* is used of God (see Psalm 119; Isaiah 45), the king (see Psalm 145:4, 7), the people (see Psalm 92:12), and individuals (see Ezekiel 18). Many uses of *righteousness* have a strong ethical undercurrent, but the best general theological definition is the one suggested by Siegfried Horn in the *SDA Bible Dictionary*.

> The state in which a right relationship exists between man and God, within the limits of man's finite comprehension of the divine will and purpose (*SDA Bible Dictionary*, p. 942).

Of special interest to our study of God's grace is a particular usage of the term *tsedeqah* and related words with which many are not familiar. Many times, righteousness refers to God's saving action. In this case, God's gracious acts in salvation are called righteousness—a true saving righteousness. Examples of this are: (1) Righteousness or vindication (*tsedeqah*) is equivalent to God's salvation (see Isaiah 61:10; 62:1, 2; 63:1). The laws of Hebrew parallelism in poetry make this clear. (2) Righteousness is the same as deliverance or victory (see Isaiah 41:2; 46:12, 13; 51:5, 6, 8). (3) "The Lord Our Righteousness" means "God our Saviour" (see Jeremiah 23:6; 33:16).

As you can see, such usage is very common in the last part of Isaiah, though it occurs in other books as well. One other place where the righteousness of God is good news is the Psalms. Examples of *tsedeqah*, or *tsadig*, as vindication or salvation or deliverance by God are: Psalms 24:5; 31:3; 51:14; 71:2, 15, 16; 98:2; 103:6, 17; 112:9; 143:11; 145:7. Psalm after psalm praises God's righteousness—His gracious, saving acts to His people. This word about God is to be treasured as gracious good news.

A Story of Grace

Martin Luther at first hated and feared the word *righteousness*. For him, it conjured up a picture of the holiness of God which could only destroy him in his unholiness.

While preparing lectures on the Psalms to give at the University, he discovered the meaning of righteousness that I have just described above. The many Psalms that portrayed God's righteousness as His gracious saving acts broke through Luther's misconceptions. God's righteousness was not a destroying holiness, but salvation for sinners!

This new understanding set Luther on the path to discovering righteousness by faith. His later study of Romans and Galations only confirmed what he had already discovered in the Old Testament psalter. The Protestant reformation was born.

God's people today need to hear the same message! How many times our misunderstanding of words has led us astray. It is time to hear God's words of grace. We need to savor them and let them awaken joy and celebration in our hearts, as they did for Luther.

14

New Testament Use of Old Testament Grace

After reading the past thirteen chapters outlining all the ways God's grace is manifested in the Old Testament, a question arises. Did anyone else see this? Could it be that this is a new, warped way of looking at the Old Testament, and the theme of grace is not here at all? The following chapter is meant to give one possible answer to that question, which is that the New Testament writers saw the Old Testament message as saying the same thing I have suggested. In particular, this chapter analyzes the apostle Paul, who is viewed by Christians as the architect of the righteousness-by-faith theology. Paul's concept of righteousness by faith is based on the Old Testament.

PAUL IN GALATIANS

Galatians, along with Romans, contains the very center of Paul's exposition of righteousness by faith. In this epistle, Paul uses the Old Testament in two major ways.

The first way is as a source of proof texts to buttress his arguments. Some of these are allusions that use only a part of the verse, like Galatians 2:16, where it appears Paul uses a phrase from Psalm 143:2 to show that people are not justified by observing the law. In other places, he quotes all or most of a verse to make his point. An example of this is Galatians 3:6, where Paul quotes Genesis 15:6, which states that Abraham's belief led God to credit him with righteousness. All in all, the Aland/Black edition of the Greek text of Galatians lists eleven direct quotations from the Old Testament. Most are used in his exposition of the gospel.

The second way Paul uses the Old Testament is probably even more important than the first. Paul deals with people and events in the Old Testament as proof for his doctrine of righteousness by faith. There are at least three of these.

The first one is the story of Abraham in Galatians 3:6-14. His argument is basically this: Abraham was righteous by faith, according to the Old Testament. All who believe, then, are "children" of Abraham because they are doing the same thing as Abraham—believing. God proclaimed this in the Old Testament because He foresaw that all nations would be blessed through Abraham. Keeping the law does *not* save. That comes only through faith, and all who have faith like Abraham's can join in that blessing of salvation.

The second major section is Galatians 3:15-25. In this section, Paul argues that the promises to Abraham were given 430 years *before* the giving of the law at Sinai. Since these promises came first and cannot be set aside, they are the true way people are saved—not by law. The law is valuable, but not as a saving instrument. It can never destroy the promises that came earlier and were based on righteousness by faith.

The third major Old Testament story Paul uses in his exposition of righteousness by faith is the story of Hagar and Sarah and their two sons found in Galatians 4:21-31. Paul points out that Hagar's son Ishmael was born in the normal way. Sarah's son, however, was born as the result of promise—as a gift of God. The two women and their sons represent two covenants. One of these covenants bears slave children in a normal way. The other bears free children of promise and God's grace. Paul's hearers are, he says, like Isaac, *not* Ishmael. They are sons of promise, not natural sons. They are sons by grace, not sons by human effort.

Importantly *all three of these stories are Old Testament stories* and are used by Paul as key elements in his argument for righteousness by faith. Clearly Paul thought the Old Testament was based on grace and taught the doctrine of righteousness by faith.

ROMANS

Romans, which contains Paul's most systematic and complete exposition of his righteousness-by-faith doctrine, is filled with Old Testament references. According to my count, there are fifty-eight quotations in the sixteen chapters of Romans as found in the Aland/Black Greek text. Many of these quotes are lengthy and go on for several verses. I simply point out a few of the places where the Old Testament plays a key role in Paul's exposition of righteousness by faith.

Most commentators see Paul's thesis statement in Romans as 1:16, 17. In this passage, he says that he's not ashamed of the gospel because it is God's power to save everyone who believes. It reveals a righteousness that is by faith from first to last. As a climax to this statement, Paul quotes Habakkuk 2:4 as evidence for this. "The righteous will live by faith." Debate has raged as to whether Paul's use of Habakkuk 2:4 is methodologically correct. Whether it is or not is, to a large extent, beside the point. It is clear that for Paul, his very thesis about righteousness by faith is firmly grounded in the Old Testament. For him the Old Testament testifies clearly to righteousness by faith.

As one goes on, it seems almost as if Paul's exposition of the gospel is an extended Old Testament Bible study. All of his major points are grounded in Old Testament Scripture.

Paul's belief that all are sinners is proved from the Old Testament (see Romans 4:9-18). So is the fact of God's faithfulness in spite of man's unfaithfulness (see 4:3, 4). Again,

Abraham is seen as the prime example of righteousness by faith (see 4:1-25). David also testifies to the truth of salvation by grace (see 4:6-8).

All this makes it abundantly clear that Paul's study of the Old Testament convinced him that God's method of working, as seen in Jesus Christ, was not something new. It was not an alien intrusion into his Jewish world. Jesus was, in fact, the fulfillment of the Old Testament in the sense that the acts of grace in the Old Testament were clearly displayed in the life of the Nazarene. Rather than being a book of legalism, the Old Testament in verse and story and history proclaims clearly the message of righteousness by faith. It is a tragedy that many modern Christians have forgotten that.

A STORY OF GRACE

It's happened so many times I should have learned my lesson. Too often I look at the package rather than at its content. I judge the inside by the outside and the quality by the wrapping. Mistakes are made.

When I saw her come to class, I wondered why she was there. She never said a word. Her heavy makeup singled her out from other girls in the class. I became uneasy because I assumed she was ill at ease in a religion class specifically geared to help students learn ways to draw closer to God.

Then the first paper came in—a description of each student's own spiritual journey. I was amazed at the depth and sincerity of what I found. I was moved to find out her decision to be a Christian had been made in the face of family opposition. I was touched to discover she was at a Christian school at financial sacrifice—her own. Subsequent papers only added to those first impressions. How wrong I had been.

Some Gentiles in Paul's day were undoubtedly amazed at Paul's expositions of God's love and grace based on the Old Testament. Their impression of some Jews they knew would have probably led them to wonder if there was anything in the Jewish holy book except law. Many Christians today need to look again at the Old Testament. They need to have new eyes—to see beyond the outward appearance they've been taught about. They will find that they have misjudged on the basis of appearance and that the inward truth taught is a message of grace. Paul himself can help them discover that.

V

Responses to Grace

To this point in the book, I have attempted to picture God's grace in the Old Testament from many different perspectives. The repetition of the same tune played from many different instruments is designed to make that tune so clear and unforgettable that God's grace is not simply accepted as a doctrine by the head but is also known in the heart and sung by the emotions.

The time has come to take the next step. When grace is accepted, what is supposed to happen? How does one respond to grace? If it really is grace—undeserved and not earned or paid for—what can the receiver do to acknowledge its reception?

In this section, I suggest what I believe are the three major responses to grace that the Old Testament teaches. They are: (1) joyous worship; (2) persistent remembrance; and (3) loving obedience. A chapter is devoted to each of these. They are *not* mutually exclusive but join and interlock together to form a united response to the tremendous gift of grace that has been freely given.

15

Worship and Celebration

Worship has been rightly called the forgotten jewel of God's people. No set of printed Bible studies or doctrinal books that I know of really gives it the place it deserves or the attention it receives in the Bible. Worship is the number one response of people when touched by the grace and presence of God. The first thing people in the Bible do when they see God's grace is worship. It precedes and is more crucial than *any* other reaction. It also forms the *basis* and source of all other proper responses.

In this chapter, I attempt to do three things. First, demonstrate that worship is the number one way people respond to God; second, attempt to define and explain worship; and third, show why the Bible makes it so important.

THE PRIORITY OF WORSHIP

The top priority of worship is shown in many ways. The first is by example. In story after story in which God acts graciously, the natural response of the people involves worship and praise.

This was true for Abraham. God gave him the promise of the land of Canaan, and when he arrived, the first thing he did was build an altar (see Genesis 12:7). Time and again, Abraham built altars and called on the name of the Lord (see Genesis 12:8; 13:18; 22:9). There were times when he returned to previous altars and prayed in the name of the Lord (see Genesis 13:4). Although sacrifice on the altar is not specifically mentioned, it is probably implied. "Calling on the name of the Lord" would certainly include prayer but would probably include other formal acts of worship as well. While we might wish for greater details of what he did, it is clear that he responded to God in worship.

The same priority for worship is shown in the story of the Exodus. When the Egyptians were destroyed in the sea, the people "feared" the Lord (see Exodus 14:31, NIV). *Fear* is used in some instances to define reverence or worship, but it is not necessary to press the definition here. Why not? Because the first tangible thing the people did after their rescue was to sing the great song of Moses in praise to the Lord. The song in Exodus 15 praises and extols God for His great deliverance. After Moses and presumably the other men finished their song (see Exodus 15:1-18), Miriam took a tambourine and led all the women in a song of praise, accompanied by music and dancing (see Exodus 15:19-21). The initial response to God's great Exodus deliverance was a song of worship and praise.

Over and over again in the Old Testament, we see the same pattern. Altars and other places of worship, sacrifices, and songs of worship and praise are the basic ways people responded to God's goodness.

The priority of worship is also shown by the commands and instructions God gave. The first four of the ten commandments in Exodus 20 all relate to worship. The first commandment says that only one God is to be worshiped. The second commandment says *how* this one God is to be worshiped—with no idols or images. The third commandment speaks against the misuse of the Lord's name. The Lord's name represents the Lord Himself, and profaning or misusing His name destroys true worship. The fourth commandment makes the Sabbath holy or special—a thing to be reverenced.

If all the laws and regulations of the Old Testament were counted and measured by number and words used, it would be clear that laws relating to worship would outnumber *all* others. Think how much time is spent describing the worship in the tabernacle and all the sacrifices and rituals connected with it. These things all relate to the worship of God.

The priority of worship is also demonstrated by the amount of time the Bible spends on the subject. It is seen as the predominant religious activity of the believer although it is hard to count because of the tremendous variety of terms and phrases used to describe it. I think most would not argue with this statement, though figures might vary widely. The best proof of this is the Psalms—both the longest book of the Old Testament and the praise and worship book of Israel.

DEFINITION OF WORSHIP

The centrality of worship in the experience of Israel is described in a number of ways. Because of this there is no simple definition of worship. In an attempt to define it, I will do three things: (1) define the key words; (2) point out other words and phrases that are used in connection with worship; and (3) describe the key characteristics of worship.

The two Hebrew words that most often are translated *worship*—*shachah* and *saqad*—both mean literally "to bow down or prostrate oneself." In the typical picturesque Hebrew way, these words depict a physical action. The most basic element of worship is the literal act of prostration.

A multitude of other words and phrases clearly relate to worship. Some of the words are *reverence, glorify, honor, praise* (there are actually three Hebrew words for *praise*), *magnify, bow down, fear, bless* (especially the Lord and/or His name), *extol, adore*, and *give thanks*. Some of the phrases are: *seek the Lord's face, offer sacrifices to the Lord, sing or make melody to the Lord, stand in the Lord's presence*, and the list could go on. If you read the Psalms carefully in various versions, you can make your own list. All of these words in some way define or describe our worship.

A study of the passages on worship leads us to certain key characteristics that help us understand what it is.

1. *Worship is basically a verb—usually involving an action.* Bowing down, kneeling, standing, sacrificing, singing, playing instruments, clapping, raising hands, and shouting praises are all parts of worship. True worship in the Old Testament sense is holistic—involving mind *and* body as the total person responds to God. This means that worship is *participatory.* It is not a spectator sport in which placid observers analyze what is going on. To worship is to be actively engaged in responding to and reaching out for God.

2. *Worship is in the first and second person—direct and close—rather than in the third person—indirect and distant.* Old Testament singers of praise did at times talk *about* God, but that was, by and large, only the prelude to singing *to* God. Note the Exodus 15 song "*I* will sing to the Lord." "The Lord is *my* strength." "*Your* right hand, O Lord, was majestic in power." The Psalms are the same way. The address of praise was to God directly. Singers sang not as a performance to the audience but as an offering of praise to God. They sang as a lover to his beloved, not as a special soloist before a panel of judges.

3. *Time is taken for worship.* Worship is not a preliminary to anything. It is important in itself. It is not to be hastily finished so the program can move along. Worship is the essence of relationship with God and central to the experience of the believer. To have worshiped is to have done that which is most important. Worshiping is no more a waste of time for the lover of God than is strolling hand in hand in the moonlight to sweethearts.

4. *Music is often a key element in worship.* The use of music, by voice and instruments of all kinds, is mentioned often in the Psalms. Music in all the ways it can be made is enlisted in the praise of God. Any examination of church history reveals that every renewal in Christianity has been accompanied by

new songs with which joyful hearts sing the message of God's love and grace.

Although composed of many elements, worship can be understood. True understanding is not, however, only intellectual. Real worship can only take place in the person whose *heart* knows and responds because it has been set alight by the mercy and grace of God.

WHY IS WORSHIP CRUCIAL?

Worship by its very nature is the only appropriate response to grace. Grace is something undeserved and unearned. It can't be purchased or merited even though God's favor is the most valuable treasure in the world. Any response other than worship would destroy the nature of the gracious gift.

I'm thankful for my teaching job. I love to teach, but each time I receive my paycheck I don't go down and worship the college financial vice-president whose signature appears on the check. Managing finances is his job. He is supposed to give checks to pay wages. I've also earned those wages by my teaching. There is a sense in which I deserve my pay. Although a thank-you might be nice, the very nature of the transaction makes it inappropriate to worship him, and he doesn't expect it.

On the other hand, if I'm a sinful slave in Egypt, unable to help myself and deserving of nothing, then my deliverance is a cause for worship. Grace is in operation, and worship becomes appropriate. If I am a sinner and can't save myself, my salvation by grace gives rise to worship.

People have often asked me how to tell if they or anyone else really understands grace or has experienced righteousness by faith. The answer I most often give is how they feel about the Deliverer. If their heart is filled with love and adoration for Jesus, if they love to speak and sing His praises, if they feel like bowing before Him with tears in their eyes, they have understood grace. They know they have received a free, undeserved gift, and they delight to worship the Giver from the heart.

Worship is the priority response to grace because it alone

preserves the glorious nature of that grace. Only those who worship know the true character of God's grace.

A STORY OF GRACE

They asked me to teach the Sabbath School lesson to the juniors. Since it was Thanksgiving, we had guests from out of town, and I thought, "Why do this lesson myself? I'll recruit two other people, and we'll dramatize this story of Lazarus's resurrection in a three- or four-act play. The juniors ought to like that."

We practiced early Sabbath morning in my office. We laughed and joked as we planned our dialogue and roles. Suddenly we came to the central scene. Jesus comes to the tomb and summons Lazarus to come forth. The form of Lazarus emerges from the tomb. Suddenly Stefan, who was playing Lazarus, stopped us and got very serious. "I can't help but believe," he said, "that a man brought from death to life would fall on his face at the feet of Jesus and worship Him."

We all became silent and instantly knew it was true. In the drama of reliving the resurrection, we knew that the only natural, appropriate response was worship. I learned a lesson that day I've never forgotten. Those who experience grace, worship! Interestingly enough, although the story in John says nothing about worship, *The Desire of Ages* clearly says it took place. It's the most natural response there is. This is always true for those who experience grace.

16

Remember!

The Old Testament is filled with the importance of remembering. The Hebrew word *zakar* is used over 230 times in one form or another. Close to 50 times it appears in the imperative form as the command to remember.

Two forms of memory were seen as crucial in the Old Testament. First, it was very important that God remembered His people Israel. Second, they, as His people, had to remember Him and His works for them as a vital part of their religious experience. Whenever God performs a gracious act for His people, He desires that they remember Him and His salvation.

Remembering is important because Israel's God acted to save His people in history. That was the primary way God made Himself known. If God revealed Himself by that means, Israel needed to remember those deeds, or she would lose her identity.

The remembering God called Israel to do in response to His grace was special. It was not simply a mental record of past events. Such a definition is weak by biblical definitions. Three critical concepts are connected with remembering in the Bible. Those three concepts form the outline followed in this chapter.

MEMORY AND ACTION

Remembering in the Old Testament is never just a mental recall of an image, scene, or group of words. Memory changes a person and leads him to sense, feel, and act.

In this connection, the statement of Exodus 2:24, 25 is helpful. "God heard their groaning and he remembered his covenant with Abraham, with Isaac and with Jacob. So God looked on the Israelites and was concerned about them."

God's remembering of the covenant leads to concern for Israel. Immediately following in this passage is the story of the choice of Moses as deliverer and God's subsequent deliverance of Israel. Remembering leads to concern and saving action.

Exodus 20:8 commands Israel to remember the Sabbath day by keeping it holy.Verses 9 and 10 tell what must be done to keep it holy. The day is to be one of rest for the Israelites, and no work is to be done. Remembering the Sabbath involves more than just calling it to mind. It is a call to keep it holy and behave a certain way.

The Sabbath command in Deuteronomy 5 also uses the word *remember* in verse 15.

> Remember that you were slaves in Egypt and that the Lord your God brought you out of there with a mighty hand and an outstretched arm. Therefore the Lord your God has commanded you to observe the Sabbath day.

God here called Israel to remember His gracious deliverance of them from Egyptian slavery. This remembering meant that they were to observe the Sabbath. To keep the Sabbath is thus a form of remembering God's salvation.

One of the most powerful chapters on remembering is Deuteronomy 8. My New International Version study Bible actually calls the chapter "Do Not Forget the Lord." Although the word *remember* only occurs twice in the chapter (see verses 2, 18), the problem of forgetting is mentioned three times (see verses 11, 14, 19), and the whole chapter is a treatise on the meaning of remembering and the tragedy of forgetting. It is clear in this passage that remembering means recalling all God's goodness and acting on it by observing His commands, walking in His ways, and reverencing Him (see verse 6). Forgetting means pride, trust in your own strength and wealth, worshiping other gods, and disobeying God's commands. Forgetting ultimately leads to destruction (see verse 19).

Response to God's gracious acts means to remember them, i.e., act on them in love, loyalty, and service to God.

REMEMBERING AS RETELLING

One key way to remember God's acts is to retell them constantly. This is done by repeating them to our children and others, learning the words and having them in prominent places, and building memorials to the acts of God.

The first two of these—the retelling of the story and the learning of the words—are specifically dealt with in Deuteronomy 6. Verses 20-23 say that when one's child asks the reason for God's laws, the parents are to retell the Exodus salvation story. The telling of the deliverance story—"remembering" it—is the reason for commandment keeping.

The same theme is echoed in Deuteronomy 32:7. "Remember the days of old; consider the generations long past. Ask your father and he will tell you, your elders, and they will explain to you."

We remember by repeating across the generations the same story.

Remembering also takes place by a constant reminding.

> Impress them on your children. Talk about them when you sit at home and when you walk along the road, when you lie down and when you get up. Tie them as symbols on your hands and bind them on your foreheads. Write them on the door frames of your houses and on your gates (Deuteronomy 6:7, 8).

Little tangible reminders in all parts of life and at all times help us remember.

Concrete memorials to specific deeds of God are also important ways to retell, and thus remember, what God has done. When Israel, because of God's gracious intervention, crossed the Jordan into Canaan on dry ground, the Lord told Joshua to gather twelve stones—one for each of the twelve tribes. The purpose of these stones was

> to serve as a sign among you. In the future, when your children ask you, "What do these stones mean?" tell them that the flow of the Jordan was cut off before the ark of the covenant of the Lord. . . . These stones are to be a memorial to the people of Israel forever (Joshua 4:6, 7).

Such memorials stood as perpetual signs retelling again and again the story of grace and calling for remembrance. They served as sites for pilgrimages—places where the story could live again.

REMEMBERING BY RITUAL AND CELEBRATION

Another way to remember God's acts is to use celebration and ritual. The great feasts of Israel are marvelous examples of this kind of remembering. While in a sense they are also retellings and memorials to God's grace, in some ways they go beyond that. There is a very real sense in which they not only tell the story but recreate and reenact the event so that participants relive the salvation of God.

Deuteronomy 16:1-3 is particularly instructive on this point. First, it should be noted that the Passover instructions here, as elsewhere, involve a mimicking of the original Passover experience. The memorial service itself copies the actual experience.

Second, throughout this passage, the deliverance from Egypt is referred to in the second person, i.e., "God . . . brought *you* out of Egypt. *You* left Egypt" (emphasis supplied). According to the record of the generation who actually left Egypt in the Exodus, only those under age twenty at the time the spies returned actually remained. Most of the Israelites who actually crossed over into Canaan didn't literally come out of Egypt. However, according to Israelite thinking, they had! If their fathers and grandfathers hadn't come out, they wouldn't be there! In a sense, then, they did come out. The celebration of the Passover affirmed their unity with the past generation and renewed the same experience for them.

Thus while the Passover was clearly a "remembering" (see Deuteronomy 16:3), it was a special kind of remembering. A participatory reenactment that in a powerful way affirmed God's grace in both past and present.

With all of these things in mind, no wonder a major response to God's grace was remembering. We who are twentieth-century people should pay careful heed to this. We live in a century that has often lost its memory. Those who forget are those who cease to exist. Those who fail to remember are, in fact, failing to respond to God's grace. We need a renewal in the church of remembering in all the ways the Old Testament talks so clearly about.

A STORY OF GRACE

Emmanuel Ringblum was a Polish historian. He belonged to a group of Jewish historians who were called the "young historians." They did brilliant work on the history of Jews in Eastern Europe.

When the Germans invaded Poland in 1939, Ringblum was not home in Poland, but in Switzerland. Despite warnings, he determined to go back to Warsaw.

"It's going into the furnace," they said. "Why do you want to go?"

"I'm a historian," he said. "I must be there when all this happens!" So he went back and made his way to the Warsaw ghetto. There he organized people, sent emissaries to all parts of the city, and coordinated resistance to the Nazis. Everyone reported to him, and he recorded it all carefully. When the Warsaw ghetto rebellion was crushed, he perished along with all the others. All of the records were buried. They were found after the war. They provided vivid insight into all that happened day by day and week by week in the ghetto so that our subsequent generation could know and remember.

In this case a serious commitment to remembering led to the death of Ringblum, but it also made the story live. God's commitment to remember is the same. He was willing to go to any length to remember us. Remembering is a key response to those who know God's grace.

17

Obey!

When most Christians think of a response to grace, obedience to God is what probably comes to mind first. Surprising as it may seem, there is really no specific word in Hebrew for *obedience* or *obey*. The word translated *obey* is the word *shama* or *hear*. The noun *obedience* really doesn't occur. *Obey* is a form of the word *hear*. The word occurs 1,136 times in the Old Testament. Sometimes translators struggle over how it should be translated. In the KJV it is rendered *obey* or *hearken* about a fourth of the time and as *hear* the remaining times. A careful study of the word yields helpful insights.

PREREQUISITES FOR OBEDIENCE

The call to obey is based on two basic prerequisites. The first is the right to command. Before a person is ready to obey, he must be convinced that the one commanding has the authority to issue the command. If that is lacking, there is no reason to obey. This principle is clearly illustrated in Pharaoh's response when Moses issued Yahweh's command to Pharaoh to let His people go. "Pharaoh said, 'Who is the Lord, that I should obey him and let Israel go? I do not know the Lord and I will not let Israel go' " (Exodus 5:2). God's gracious acts to Israel revealed who He was and what His power could do.

On the basis of this knowledge of God, the call to obey can be issued. However, those who don't know God need this revelation as a basis for their obedience.

The second prerequisite for obedience is a knowledge of what God wants. He must in some way reveal His will so that individuals can know precisely what God expects of them.

In the Old Testament, man-to-God obedience is usually spoken of in one of two ways. In many cases people are called to obey the voice of God or the word of God. The idea is that God has spoken and declared Himself, and man is to follow in response to that divine word. In other cases, obedience is said to be to God's commands, ordinances, or laws. Both the voice and the commands of God are treasured because they reveal His will. In other places that do not specifically mention ordinance or commandment, the Israelite was simply called to obey God—God just said, "Obey me." "I gave them this command: Obey me, and I will be your God and you will be my people. Walk in all the ways I command you, that it may go well with you" (Jeremiah 7:23).

It is interesting to note that this verse declares that God did not just give commands about offerings and sacrifices but also the simple command—"Obey *me*."

Not only does this verse make obedience a personal response to God, it also puts it in the context of a relationship with God. Personal obedience to God establishes a special bond between the two parties, and that bond bears good fruit. Disobedience destroys a personal relationship. This is why it is serious.

PARTS IN THE OBEDIENCE PACKAGE

Careful analysis of what is involved in obedience, reveals a package containing at least three major parts. The first is the actual physical *hearing*. The one expected to obey needs to actually hear and know what is being required. The second step is *trust* and *faith*. The hearer must believe that the "commander" is an authority who is to be trusted and who has the status to deserve obedience. The third part of the package is the *obedient action*. To obey means to do or follow the word or command of the "commander."

The second step is a very interesting one. It means that obedience and faith in the biblical sense are closely related terms. Despite what many think, they are not opposites. The following text bears this out: " 'Return, faithless Israel,' declares the Lord. . . . 'Only acknowledge your guilt—you have rebelled against the Lord your God, . . . and have not obeyed me. . . . Return, faithless people' " (Jeremiah 3:12-14).

This passage points out Israel's sin clearly—she had rebelled and not obeyed—but this sin earned her the adjective *faithless* twice. To sin and be disobedient is the same as faithlessness. Obedience and faith, then, are synonymous.

Genesis 22:15-18 says that Abraham's willingness to go to Moriah and sacrifice his son Isaac was an act of *obedience* by which he was blessed. Hebrews 11:17 suggests Abraham acted by *faith*. Superficially one could ask, "Well, which was it?" The answer is both because here again obedience is equated with faith. No one really obeys unless he believes in the one who gives the word or command.

Obedience, then, is not some isolated legalistic act. It fits together with a whole complex of ideas that are all a personal response to God. "Who among you fears the Lord and obeys the word of his servant? Let him who walks in the dark, who has no light, trust in the name of the Lord and rely on his God" (Isaiah 50:10). This passage implies that to fear the Lord, to obey Him, to trust Him, and to rely on Him are all related ideas.

Deuteronomy suggests the same idea by associating the theme of loving the Lord and holding fast to Him with that of obedience:

> I have set before you life and death, blessings and curses.

> Now choose life, so that you and your children may live and that you may love the Lord your God, listen to his voice [better translated *obey*], and hold fast to him. For the Lord is your life (Deuteronomy 30:19, 20).

Love, faith, and obedience in the Old Testament all define a heart response to the God who graciously saves and cares for His people.

Obedience, then, can best be defined as an action based on an understanding of God and a trusting belief that He has spoken and is who He claims to be. It is not some legalistic following of an abstract code, but a response of the whole person to the living, loving God. As such, it forms a worthy partner with worship and remembrance as an appropriate response to God's grace.

It is certainly this type of obedience Paul had in mind in Romans 1:5 when he talks about "the obedience that comes from faith." Paul knew his Old Testament well. He was not propounding a new idea but rephrasing the Old Testament view well. True obedience is even now an act of faith. Those who have experienced God's grace delight to obey Him.

A STORY OF GRACE/OBEDIENCE

In Chiang Mai, Thailand, we lived next to the church on a busy road leading to a famous mountain temple shrine. On the other side was a famous Thai klong, or canal, about thirty feet wide. It was actually part of the old moat that originally surrounded the ancient walled city. Our yard was large, and our children had plenty of room to play. My wife was usually closely watching them as well.

One day Kathy thought she would play it especially safe. She locked the large gate at the side of the road to make sure the children didn't stray onto the street or fall into the klong. She turned her back for just an instant, and when she looked back at the children, she panicked. Agile 2-1/2-year-old Paul had found enough space under the gate to get outside the fence and stood fascinated at the roadside, looking longingly at the "swimming pool" across the road. The key to the gate was upstairs in the house, and the space under the gate was too small for Kathy to crawl under. Scared to death, she ran to the gate and begged Paul to obey and come back under the gate. He seemed amused by the whole thing, but lingered there by the gate long enough for someone to get the key and open it. He "listened" to his mother long enough to be saved. He believed in her enough not to venture farther. Do we listen and believe God that much?

CONCLUSION

Worshiping, remembering, and obeying are not three steps in responding to God's grace. Neither are they three separate entities. They are closely related ideas linked together like three interlocking circles or like different facets of one diamond. Together they form a natural response to God's grace. All three taken together might form a practical definition of faith.

VI

Objections to Old Testament Grace

The concluding section of this book is written for those who may say that I've been too selective. I can hear it now! "You have picked all the nice passages that portray God's grace. What about all the other stuff? Aren't you going to admit there is another side?" These last several chapters are meant to answer questions about God's grace.

In some ways, I rebel against writing this chapter. Who is God that He needs defending, and who am I to attempt to explain the Almighty? For most believers, this section is unnecessary. They have already come to terms with God. Most unbelievers will probably not be convinced by what I propose. However, in hopes that perhaps some may have their faith strengthened and a few honest questioners may be helped, this section is offered.

18

Is the Old Testament Legalistic?

The basic thesis of this book is that the way God saved people in the Old Testament is exactly the same way He did in the New—by grace. Righteousness by faith is the way of salvation in both testaments.

The first and most natural objection to this thesis is that it is not true. The Old Testament, many would claim, is a legalistic book. The way of salvation taught there is righteousness by works. People in the Old Testament were taught that good works brought them standing with God. This objection is a serious one, and proof texts can be produced that seem to support it. This chapter attempts to answer this issue.

TEXTS USED FOR LEGALISM

Numerous texts could be used by those arguing for the legalistic view of Old Testament religion. I quote an example:

> See, I am setting before you today a blessing and a curse—the blessing if you obey the commands of the Lord your God that I am giving you today; the curse if you disobey the commands of the Lord your God and turn from the way that I command you today by following other gods (Deuteronomy 11:26-28).

Blessings are promised for obedience, and a curse for disobedience. Many see this as a simple statement that salvation (blessing) comes to those who obey, while damnation (curse) comes on those who disobey. If this interpretation is followed, many other similar texts can be used to say the same thing.

Other types of passages that seem to teach legalism are those that define righteousness as doing certain things and then seeing that as the way to life. A prime example is Ezekiel 18. Verses 5 to 9 give an extended catalog of what righteous deeds are. They define a righteous man as one who does not eat at mountain shrines, look at idols, defile his neighbor's wife, oppress anyone, commit robbery, and the list goes on. The passage concludes, "He follows my decrees and faithfully keeps my laws. That man is righteous; he will surely live, declares the Sovereign Lord" (Ezekiel 18:9).

A similar, though opposite, list describes the unrighteous man. The passage concludes: "Will such a man live? He will not! Because he has done all these detestable things, he will surely be put to death and his blood will be on his own head" (Ezekiel 18:13).

Some would argue that righteousness is doing these things, and it leads to life (salvation), while unrighteousness is doing certain other things that lead to death (damnation). This would teach that even the Old Testament prophets thought people were saved by their righteous deeds—by their law keeping.

If one wanted to demonstrate this theology from a historical example, the near sacrifice of Isaac would be a good choice. After Abraham obeyed God by traveling to Mount Moriah to attempt to sacrifice Isaac, God renewed His powerful covenant promise to Abraham.

> I swear by myself, declares the Lord, that because you have done this and have not withheld your son, your only son, I will surely bless you and make your descendants as numerous as the stars in the sky. . . . Through your offspring all nations on earth will be blessed, because you have *obeyed* me (Genesis 22:15-18, emphasis supplied).

This promise comes, some would argue, on the basis of what Abraham has done—he has obeyed. Abraham is righteous by his deeds, not by his faith.

How does one answer these questions?

A LOOK AT THE BROAD CONTEXT

I suggest that reading these passages in their broad context—in their setting in Israel—shows that they do not teach legalism. An examination of historical and literary context follows, which seeks to demonstrate that fact.

The Deuteronomy text, or any that teach similar ideas, follows historically *after* grace has already been received. The basic salvation for the Israelites in their deliverance from Egyptian slavery had already taken place when Deuteronomy was written. They stood at the edge of Canaan as God's own people by grace. This deliverance took place, not because Israel was great and earned it, but because God loved her. What Deuteronomy records is *post*salvation. God had already established the Israelites as His people. In that relationship, things would go well (blessings) if they obeyed, and would not go well (curses) if they didn't. The call to obey was not a way of establishing the relationship between God and Israel; rather, it was a way of maintaining it. It was a call, not to salvation, but to growth.

Even this call to obey is not some kind of wooden, mechanical rule. The passage in Deuteronomy 11 itself sees the call to obey as a call to allegiance, or loyalty to God. To disobey is to turn from "your God" to "following other gods" (Deuteronomy 11:28). To obey is to maintain faithfulness. In fact, in an earlier passage (see Deuteronomy 11:13), to faithfully obey the commands was basically to "love the Lord your God." The obedience called for was a love allegiance to the God who saved. That is not legalism, or righteousness by works.

Much the same thing could be said for the passage in Ezekiel. The only difference was that more time had passed. The Israelites, through persistent sin, had been taken captive in Babylon. God had not only initially established them as His people by saving them from Egyptian slavery, He also promised to again deliver them, this time from Babylonian slavery and exile. Ezekiel makes it clear that this deliverance would not be based at all on Israel's acts of goodness, but on God's gracious deeds for them (see Ezekiel 36:22-38 for a long, detailed statement of this fact). God gave His Spirit to move Israel to follow His decrees and carefully keep His law (see Ezekiel 36:27). Ezekiel 18 describes, not a way to salvation, but the way people who are already saved should live to keep their covenant with God alive.

Not only does the historical context teach this, but the literary context makes it clear as well. One theological idea that led the Israelites to feel their situation as exiles was hopeless was the concept that the sins of their ancestors had separated them from God to the point where they could do nothing about it. The basic argument in Ezekiel 18 is that the sins of their ancestors *didn't* leave them outside of God and hopeless. If one turns to God, "He will not die for his father's sin; he will surely live" (Ezekiel 18:17b). The message is one of hope. Anyone who repents and turns to God can live—past sin is forgiven. The whole passage concludes:

> O house of Israel, I will judge you, each one according to his ways, declares the Sovereign Lord. Repent! . . . Rid yourselves of all the offenses you have committed, and get a new heart and a new spirit. Why will you die, O house of Israel? For I take no pleasure in the death of anyone, declares the Sovereign Lord. Repent and live! (Ezekiel 18:30-32).

Israel's relationship with God was viewed in a much more permanent way than most twentieth-century Christians view their relationship with God. Israel's existence as a chosen people led her to have few questions about being "saved" or "not saved." She was obviously saved, in her eyes, by her very existence. Few Israelites doubted the surety of their salvation. They had assurance by their very peoplehood. When, however, at the time of Ezekiel that peoplehood was in jeopardy, what formerly had assured them now led to despair. As before, they were saved as a people; now, they were hopelessly lost as a people. This passage was God's message of hope that the sins of their fathers had not made them lose their chance of a relationship with God. That chance is, of course, a project of God's graciousness and forgiveness.

The passages dealing with Abraham, if examined carefully, also demonstrate that they do not support the legalistic viewpoint. Viewed historically, the promises given in Genesis 22 to Abraham are, at heart, a restatement of promises given earlier in Genesis 12:1-3 and Genesis 15:9-21. In an earlier chapter, the graciousness of those free promises was discussed. Abraham received these promises as God's graciousness to him.

We have also already dealt with the fact that what Genesis 22:18 calls "obedience," Hebrews 11:17 calls "faith." The two are closely related. Abraham trusted God and thus obeyed and followed Him. The promises did not come because of obedience. They had already been given. They were reaffirmed because Abraham showed he really believed God's word to him.

Read in the full context of Israel's relationship with God and His dealing with her, passages that on the surface seem legalistic turn out not to be. To call God's way of dealing with people in the Old Testament legalistic is to read it with a theological lens that distorts the text. Some Jews did become legalistic in their understanding of God. So have some Christians. This fact should not, however, cause us to read these problems into the text. These are problems with understanding, not problems with God's way of dealing with issues.

A STORY OF GRACE

As I write these words, not a week has passed since Valentine's Day. In class this morning, we talked about the commandments of God and Valentine's Day. I questioned the class about the validity of giving my wife a Valentine card and gift.

We discovered that there are numerous logical and theological reasons for not doing anything for one's beloved on Valentine's Day. Although named after a Christian martyr, the day's practices have pagan roots, and some of them are even immoral. Hearts, arrows, cupids, and silly rhymes are not only sentimental, but probably also childish. Spending money on these things is not good stewardship. Mature relationships shouldn't need artificial things like Valentine's Day to bolster them. Valentines and gifts can be manipulative. Valentines can be legalistic—people can give them because they think they have to earn a relationship. Valentines can become a meaningless ritual that enslaves a person. The list could go one and on! It is so easy to misunderstand or misuse Valentine's Day.

Did I give my wife a valentine in the light of all this evidence? Of course! In spite of all the dangers? Yes—for sure!

Why? Because I know that deep down inside she'd feel bad if I didn't. She'd be disappointed. If I persisted in purposefully passing up chances to say "I love you," she'd probably begin to wonder if I did. She wouldn't divorce me over one missed Valentine's Day, but establishing a trend like that is risky. I love her too much to take a chance like that.

Obeying God's laws is a lot like that. All kinds of risks, dangers, and misunderstanding are possible. People can obey for wrong reasons and become legalistic. But those who have felt the unmerited grace of God know deep down they want to respond, and so they do—from the heart. They know God wants it—not because they need to get married but because they *are* happily married. They desire to give a valentine to God.

19

God—a Destroyer?

In the last chapter, we briefly discussed the objection that the God of the Old Testament is a legalist. The second objection to the concept of God's grace is the destruction of people. Bluntly put, how can a gracious, loving God destroy people—not just warriors, but women, children, and animals as well? What is gracious about all this? Is God's grace only for certain people? Is He only selectively gracious? First, we'll take a look at the problem and then attempt some solutions.

DESTRUCTION IN THE OLD TESTAMENT

The Old Testament clearly portrays God as leading out in the destruction of armies that arise in opposition to His people. Examples would be Pharaoh's army at the Red Sea and Jehoshaphat's victory over Moab and Ammon in 2 Chronicles 20.

To fight against God's people, however, means to fight

against God, and that may extend beyond one battle. After Israel battled the Amalekites, God said: "I will completely erase the memory of the Amalekites from under heaven." "The Lord will be at war against the Amalekites from generation to generation" (Exodus 17:14, 16). Although this passage does not make it clear that *everyone* is to be destroyed, other passages make it clear that this is often what happened. Speaking of Jericho, the book of Joshua says, "They devoted the city to the Lord and destroyed with the sword every living thing in it—men and women, young and old, cattle, sheep and donkeys" (Joshua 6:21).

When Israel left Egypt at the Passover, God's angel destroyed all the firstborn of men and cattle (see Exodus 11:5).

Some believe that these judgements happened only to Israel's enemies. That is not true. Israelites were also subject to this kind of judgment. Their families, children, and animals were *also* at times included in the destruction. Numbers 16 records the story of the revolt of Korah, Dathan, and Abiram. These men perished when the earth opened and swallowed them. Included in the "swallowing" were their wives, little ones, and possessions. Everything of theirs went with them into the earth.

Achan's sin, recorded in Joshua 7, received the same treatment.

> Joshua, together with all Israel, took Achan son of Zerah, the silver, the robe, the gold wedge, his sons and daughters, his cattle, donkeys and sheep, his tent and all that he had. . . . Then all Israel stoned him, and after they had stoned the rest, they burned them (Joshua 7:24).

The list could go on, but enough has been said to demonstrate that both Israelites and non-Israelites, young and old, male and female, man and animal lost their lives from what the Old Testament viewed as acts of God.

Before discussing ways of dealing with this, it is important to remind people that this problem is not just an Old Testament problem. It is fallacious to pit a cruel Old Testament against a gentle New Testament. This represents a very selective reading of the text. While the Old Testament may seem more crude and blatant in places, in many ways the New Testament is actually more of a problem. Uzziah's death for a seemingly minor infringement of an ordinance is terrible, but nowhere does the Bible say that this resulted in eternal damnation. Most Old Testament passages regarded the punishment as temporal, while New Testament passages portray God's punishment as eternal! The book of Revelation is as filled with destruction as any Old Testament book. The problem that we face here, then, is a biblical problem rather than simply an Old Testament difficulty.

STEPS TOWARD A SOLUTION

In looking at these incidents and the destroying side of God, several preliminary factors need to be emphasized. First, these destroying acts are always seen as a result of the sin of the parties involved. God does not destroy people on a whim or capriciously just because He doesn't care for them. Pagan gods could do things to people just because they wanted to. Israel's God always gave a *moral* reason. If you look at the record carefully, at least the ones who led out in evil doing are seen as wrong and sinful. The specific charge is made clear.

Second, most often the sin related to some kind of threat to Israel's existence. The survival of God's people was at stake. Disciplinary actions usually were those that rescued Israel from national ruin and thus preserved a witness to the world of the true God. Actually, the Exodus; the destruction of Ammonites, Amalekites, and Canaanites; the rebellion of Korah, Dathan, and Abiram all fit this mold. The destruction is, to a large extent, then, a saving act for the righteous of Israel. To the righteous ones saved by destruction of evil, the whole story of destruction is a story of their deliverance and salvation.

The third preliminary factor is the corporate or group nature of Israel's thinking. Twentieth-century Westerners view most sins and punishments from the context of the individual. Individual sins receive individual punishment. For Israel the group was important, and individual sins affected the group.

The loss of thirty-six men in the attempted conquest of Ai was traced to the sin of Achan. It is clear that not only did Achan's sin affect Israel, the Bible implicates Achan's family in the commission of the sin also. The family of a person is seen as a very real extension of that person. The story also would imply that the family at least quietly complied with Achan. It would have been nearly impossible to have hidden all the things he took from Jericho in a hole in his tent and not have people in the family know. Because of this, Achan's household perished with him. We may not like this kind of thinking, but for Israel it was the way their world operated. None complained about what happened.

If, in fact, we look at our own system of punishment, others suffer as well. In our community of Walla Walla live many wives and children of inmates of the Washington State Penitentiary. You could not convince me that just the husbands and fathers suffer punishment. Wives struggle for jobs and community acceptance. Children suffer loneliness and stigma. The whole family suffers.

Although recognizing these factors should clarify this issue a bit, there are still questions. Doesn't this all still seem a bit harsh? True, the families may have been seen as units, but shouldn't God at least have been a bit easier on the kids? There are several major ways this issue has been dealt with through the years. I explain briefly those options and then evaluate them.

One way to deal with the issue is to either reject or neglect the Old Testament. One can declare oneself a New Testament believer and reject the Old Testament or ignore the Old Testament as inferior or dangerous. This tack has been taken both by believers and unbelievers through the centuries. For Christians one main problem with this is that the Old Testament was clearly the Word of God and an authority for Jesus and the apostles! Were they wrong?

Another view that has been popular recently is to see the whole problem stemming from the cultural milieu of Israel. As primitive former slaves they had views of God heavily influenced by their cultural setting. God was not really like that, but the only way they knew how to describe Him was in those terms. The descriptions, then, of God's acts are not to be taken literally.

While it is true that Israel's culture affected them and that the study of the Semitic worldview can be helpful, for such gross false views to be portrayed in Scripture raises other pressing questions. If something as basic as this is wrong, how can anything the Bible says about God be true? Are statements about His love and grace also only cultural?

Another popular view is the concept of progressive revelation. This places the reason for misunderstanding on God. These incidents were God's way of dealing with people who couldn't understand anything more. While it is true that God dealt with these people where they were, He has always done this. Doesn't He also deal with us where we are? Besides, if things progressed so much, why is this element in the New Testament as well as the Old? Unfortunately, many take those parts of the Old Testament that they *like* as true and those that they don't care for as the "unprogressive" or nonapplicable parts. That kind of selectivity bothers me. I believe God progressively reveals Himself, but that does not negate earlier revelations.

While seeing the value of cultural study and recognizing that God's revelation grows, I think a wholehearted dependence on either of these views alone is dangerous. The most basic question is "Why were these stories told?" What is the reason or purpose the Bible writer and God's Spirit have in preserving these stories for us?

There is in *all* these cases some underlying message that is meant to be heard. The discovery of that message is crucial to relating to the problem. I suspect that close to the heart of all of these stories is a message about the horrible, destructive nature of sin. The message is about the awesome consequences of wrong—a burden to convey the holiness of God.

I then turn to the problems, not of *their* culture, but my own. What about *my* worldview makes me wonder about God so much? Is what my society does to sinners more just? Is it really better for the families of evildoers to be minus husband

and father, and scrap for life in a world that looks down on them? Might they not be happier all together in prison, where they'd at least be equal with others and have guaranteed food and shelter? Why do I have such a hard time relating to the horrible consequences of sin? Am I realistic?

Lastly, I believe there remains a sense of mystery. I don't know all the answers. Learning to live with questions may in the end be more fruitful than arriving at final answers. I won't ever know how to explain fully *why* God seems to have behaved as He did, but He's God, and I'm man. I don't think He minds my asking, but I do believe He may not expect my human mind to fathom it all.

20

God—Unjust and Uncaring?

The two stories dealt with in this section are related to the last chapter on "God—the Destroyer." Many of the principles discussed there apply to this chapter as well. What, then, is the reason for this chapter? The incidents covered in this chapter carry the issue a bit farther. While in the last chapter we discussed God's actual destroying of people in punishment for sin, in this chapter we deal with God's leading—or seeming to lead—into or cause sin. It is one thing to punish for sin and another to lead or cause people to do the sin that results in their punishment. This chapter also deals with the issue of God's attitude toward those who sin and the seeming greater mercy of Moses, the human, over God, the divine.

HARDENING PHARAOH'S HEART

God is said to harden Pharaoh's heart nine times in Exodus 4 to 14 (see 4:21; 7:3; 9:12; 10:1, 20, 27; 11:10; 14:4, 8). Three different Hebrew words are used to describe this hardening which caused Pharaoh's stubbornness and failure to release Israel. This, in turn, led to the ten plagues that resulted in the death of firstborn males in Egypt. The question is, of course, how is it fair to lead one to sin and then punish him and his people because of it?

In fairness, it should also be pointed out that six times the book of Exodus says that Pharaoh's heart was hardened—not naming the agent of hardening (see 7:13, 14, 22; 8:19; 9:7, 35). Three times the Scriptures say that Pharaoh hardened his heart (see 8:15, 32; 9:34). In summary, then, nine times God is seen as the hardener of Pharaoh's heart, and nine times Exodus simply says Pharaoh's heart was hardened or that Pharaoh hardened his own heart.

The most interesting passage is Exodus 9:34, 35, which contains references to all three types of phrases:

> When Pharaoh saw that the rain and the hail and the thunder had ceased, *he sinned yet again, and hardened his heart*, he and his servants. So the *heart of Pharaoh was hardened*, and he did not let the people of Israel go; *as the Lord had spoken through Moses* (RSV, emphasis supplied).

This passage says first that Pharaoh sinned and hardened his heart. It continues by saying that his heart was hardened and concludes by stating that this happened according as the Lord has spoken to Moses. In Exodus 7:3 and 44:21 God promised Moses to harden Pharaoh' heart, and this phrase in Exodus 9:35 seems to recall these other verses.

This seems to imply that all three phrases are true. One does *not* rule out the other. God's hardening does not rule out a choice for Pharaoh. Pharaoh's opportunity for choice does not mean God is not working on him. The three phrases could probably be used interchangeably.

To our way of thinking, there is a major difference between *causing* an action and *allowing* it. I think that for the Hebrew mind there would have been no great difference between the two. They saw God as the real, active cause of things. We would like to see God as causing certain things, but would probably feel more comfortable if this text portrayed God as allowing this to happen. I think for Israel these were the same—or at least the results came out the same.

The Hebrew mind, then, seems to have been comfortable with a dual causality of events. Man's choice and God's action were not mutually exclusive—both could be active at the same time.

The question still remaining, though, is why God did it so many times. The answer is to make a point. The point is mentioned in Exodus 7:

> I will harden Pharaoh's heart, and though I multiply my signs and wonders in the land of Egypt, Pharaoh will not listen to you; then I will lay my hand upon Egypt and bring forth my hosts, my people the sons of Israel, out of the land of Egypt by great acts of judgment (Exodus 7:3, 4, RSV).

The hardening—and the whole Exodus story for that matter—emphasizes the saving power of God. The Exodus deliverance is His deliverance—not Pharaoh's or Moses' or Aaron's. He shows who He is and what He can do so that all may know Him. Pharaoh thinks he's the ultimate ruler, but the Exodus story proves him wrong. Yahweh is supreme, and His people are safe as they trust in Him and His salvation.

Many times we look at this Exodus story from the standpoint of the Egyptian conquerors. Pharaoh and the Egyptians had long been oppressing Israel. This hardness of heart wasn't something new. Egyptian hardness manifested in slave labor and killing babies was a long-term thing. Slaves who desperately needed deliverance needed to see the strength of their Deliverer, and this whole story tries to make that point.

MOSES AS INTERCESSOR

The second incident we need to examine is found in Exodus 32. Moses ascended the mountain to commune with God and remained there for an extended period. In his absence the restless people fell into idolatrous worship of a golden calf that Aaron, Moses' brother, made for them. Seeing their sin, God threatened to destroy them.

> "Leave me alone so that my anger may burn against them and that I may destroy them. Then I will make you into a great nation." But Moses sought the favor of the Lord his God. "O Lord," he said, "why should your anger burn against your people? (Exodus 32:10, 11).

Moses reasoned with God and reminded Him of His covenant and promise and of what the Egyptians might say. Later in the chapter, Moses volunteered to lose his life to save his people. God then relented His anger and had mercy. A similar incident occurred in Amos 7:1-6. There Amos pleaded for Israel, and God granted his request.

Is God really like that? Does He like to punish and listen to human instruments more merciful than He? How does one reconcile this with the passage just two chapters later (Exodus 34:6, RSV), which talks of this same God as merciful and gracious and slow to anger? Is God two-faced? Is God just changeable?

Several suggestions have been made to explain this passage. The first is that God designed this as a test for Moses. Moses was God's chosen leader and faced a long period of time attempting to lead a stubborn people. At that time, near the beginning of his work, God tested Moses to see if he really cared about the people. God's threat to destroy gave Moses a chance to display and develop his role as leader and intercessor with God. It also showed him how much influence he did have with God. It is possible that this explanation has some truth. My major objection is that the text does not seem to portray it in that way. If it were a test, why is it not told that way? Shouldn't there be some hint that this is so?

Another suggested explanation is that God desires to work with and deal with people where they are in their specific culture and situation. In this period of history, gods were expected to act in this way. They were supposed to get angry, etc. What God did was communicate in a way that really communicated. He acted as deity was supposed to so that Israel would really believe He was God. Again, it can be said that there is some truth in this. God does relate to people in an understandable way. There are, however, many places where He deliberately behaves differently from the other gods. How do we know which He has done at this point? Isn't this a dangerous way and place to communicate, leaving God open to all kinds of misunderstanding?

The explanation I find most satisfying attempts to explain this passage as a story reconciling the justice and mercy aspects of God. When I studied Bible doctrines, I was taught to define God in terms of certain characteristics or attitudes. Many of these attributes begin with the prefix *omni* or *im*. You've heard the list—God is omnipresent (present everywhere), omniscient (all-knowing), omnipotent (all-powerful), immutable (unchanging), immortal (undying), etc. Interestingly, by and large the Bible does not define God this way. The God so defined is a philosophical, abstract God whom I call the God of the "omnis."

Viewing God on the basis of the "omnis" leads to philosophical problems. Can God make a rock so big He can't lift it? Can God choose not to know something? Is God powerful enough to make Himself mortal? The list can go on and on. One question particularly relevant to this discussion is what does God do when justice demands one course of action and love/mercy suggests another?

The biblical picture of God differs from the doctrinal God of the "omnis." It is not that God doesn't know or can't do certain things, but that what is presented and emphasized is different. The God of the Old Testament is known by His actions. The Old Testament need not call Him omnipotent—it merely tells of His mighty deeds of creation and redemption. His omnipresence need not be stated but is clearly implied by the fact He knows about events and can interact with all creation. The biblical God is personal and dynamic. He is not a static entity but a personal, dynamic being—entering into situations and somehow changing without being changed. The most important verse in all of Exodus 32, in my estimation, is verse 14, which says "the Lord relented" (some versions say "repented") and did not bring on the threatened destruction of His people.

Numerous Old Testament passages speak of God repenting or relenting (see, for example, Genesis 6:6, 7; Jeremiah 18:8, 10; 26:13; Amos 7:3, 6; Jonah 3:10)! God does not repent of sin but changes His course of action on the basis of human actions. The God of the Old Testament really relates to and interacts with people. This real interaction means prayer, intercession, and repentance really do work! Moses could intercede and something could happen! This God has a personal face.

I am suggesting that this story brings together God's justice and mercy. The story presents both aspects and relates them to each other in one narrative. God is just in His anger—the people have sinned and deserve what is coming to them. God is merciful in His listening to the intercession of Moses and relenting. God's use of both characteristics is shown in the story, as well as how they interact with each other.

It should also be remembered that the Moses who intercedes has, in fact, been appointed to his position by God. His role as leader and intercessor comes from God. In a real sense, he is God interceding with God. Again this is a picture of the outworking of the two necessary complementary components of God. As such Moses is a type of "Christ figure" in whom God Himself is both Judge and Saviour. No one desires a merciful but unjust God—neither does anyone want a just but unmerciful God. This story vividly pictures both these attributes in a powerful way.

VII
Conclusion

I do not pretend that the answers suggested in this chapter or the other two in this section of the book are exhaustive and answer all the questions. They don't do so for me. I continue to wonder about many things. I still wish some things weren't there and some explanations now absent could be present. I'm quite sure the mystery will continue. The main thing I have learned is to doubt my questions and doubts. My questions at times are clearer statements of *my* problems than they are testimonies to problems in the Old Testament. The question as to *why* I have certain questions has often helped me more than supposed answers to these questions. I invite you to think about such issues for yourself and continue your search for the God who is much, much bigger than all of us.

21

What New Testament Christians Can Learn About Righteousness by Faith in the Old Testament

I set out in this book to show how the Old Testament speaks the same message of righteousness by faith or God's grace as the New Testament. I hope I've been successful! I am a Christian and do believe that the fullest revelation of God is in His Son Jesus. However, Christians must realize that God didn't get merciful all of a sudden in the first century A.D. Jesus didn't come in a vacuum but was the capstone on a long history of God's mercy.

In this concluding chapter, I take one more step. I suggest that the Old Testament portrayal of righteousness by faith has in it certain emphases that a strictly New Testament presentation can miss. Thus, the Old Testament presentation of grace not only lays the foundation for the New Testament and Jesus, but can also actually help fill out the picture and give certain insights that can make the presentation of God's grace even more powerful. I do not suggest that the New Testament lacks these things, but they are often downplayed or missed in typical presentations of grace based on the New Testament.

STORY, RITUAL, AND SONG VERSUS TERM DEFINITION

Because of our past history and traditions, much of the present-day Christian church has depended heavily on definition of terms and concepts in its explanations of God's grace. As a young person, I often despaired of ever understanding righteousness by faith because I couldn't really understand the terms. *Sanctification* and *justification* were hard to define. The experts weren't even sure what they meant, so how could I, a struggling nonexpert, ever grasp it all? Faith, conversion, new birth, etc., all seemed a bit fuzzy. If salvation depended in some way on figuring all this out, I knew I was in trouble.

When people tried to outline steps to salvation, it got even worse. Had I really repented? How often did one need to repent? How could I know God accepted me? Were we sure of the order of these steps to salvation?

The Old Testament portrayal of grace emphasizes not terms and concepts but stories—stories of the Exodus, stories of people like Abraham, and stories of battles won. Stories are concrete and understood by all.

The Old Testament stresses rituals like the Passover and sacrifices and holy days. These all deal with tangible things done and experienced.

The Old Testament glories in songs of praise—psalms that don't always explain how but simply rejoice in the unexplainable, unmerited grace of God.

Such things are not only easier for most to grasp, they also do more. They enable a person to enter into and reexperience his salvation. They lead to celebration. They not only teach and inform, but they also inspire. Our presentation of righteousness by faith must learn to incorporate these elements as well.

Now, the New Testament has stories, rituals, and songs.

The prime story is, of course, the story of Jesus. Baptism and communion are rituals of salvation. The problem is that in the *presentation* of the message, these parts are often downplayed. While Paul is crucial, we must not fail to see the story, the celebration, and the song as bona fide, clear, and valuable ways to declare the good news of God's grace.

THE RICH VARIETY OF PORTRAYALS OF GRACE

Although the above section already mentions this factor, it merits further elaboration. The vast variety of ways the Old Testament speaks of God's grace can help us enrich our presentation of righteousness by faith.

Somehow, along with my earlier hangups on definition and concepts, I also imbibed another idea. That is, there was basically one way to explain righteousness by faith and God's grace. One not only had to understand certain terms, but these terms and the process of how they all worked was quite cut and dried. There was one process that led to salvation, just as there was one gate into the sheepfold.

The Old Testament can help convince us that there are many ways to explain what happens. Not all go through exactly the same process. Abraham's experience was not equal to David's. The very fact that battles teach God's grace would imply that all kinds of things in life, if viewed properly, teach His grace. One can say there are numerous stories and metaphors that speak of God's mercy, not one. There are many stories and processes leading to the gate of salvation. The New Testament itself uses many ways of explaining God's mercy. Metaphors abound—it is like being released from bondage in slavery; Jesus is a ransom; we are adopted into God's family; we are declared not guilty in court; and the list could go on. The Old Testament simply helps to push us in the direction of admitting that God's grace is so big that one story or metaphor is not sufficient. The more ways we can tell the story, the more likely we are to reach different people. The wise proclaimer of the message of grace finds that particular story or metaphor that fits most appropriately the condition of the one in need.

THE KEY ROLE OF WORSHIP

As discussed earlier in this volume, the first and most basic response to God's grace in the Old Testament is worship. Worship is the only possible response when one recognizes what grace really is—something totally undeserved. Worship, then, is the evidence, the gauge that shows one has grasped grace. Those who do not worship, then, don't know what grace is or have not responded to it.

This is also something that I failed to grasp for a long time. I thought you responded to grace by understanding and believing. The understanding was some kind of mental assent, and this was the believing. You said something like, "I now understand this in my mind, and now I assent to it and accept it as a belief." This is, of course, not totally false, but by itself is incomplete and possibly deceptive. It turns the whole thing into a doctrine or creed and can divorce the mind from the rest of the person.

The Old Testament stresses not the mental process but the whole-person response. That is, in fact, what worship is—the whole person singing, kneeling, praising, and shouting over the glorious gifts given. The mind is certainly involved but so is a whole lot more.

I happen to believe that worship is one of the greatest builders of true faith there is, to truly worship with a group that has experienced the grace of God and knows it personally changes you. The grace praised becomes more real in praising.

The New Testament does see worship as a response to God's grace. Jesus' first commandment is to love God with all the heart. Paul often breaks into doxologies in his letters. In Revelation, heaven is clearly portrayed as a place of praise. In our rush to include obedience and service to others in our response to God, we have forgotten the very *first* response. We are cleansed lepers who need to come back and fall at Jesus' feet and thank Him before we do anything else.

For me, it was the Old Testament that in clear tones urged me to worship, praise, and celebrate the goodness of God. Songs of praise and thanksgiving are not the preliminary warm-up to something else. They are of the essence of what response to God and the purpose of religious services really is. Those who worship and celebrate grace receive more. Those who fail to worship have not grasped that grace and must stumble on, trying to earn their way. Is it any wonder that the renewal message given to our church begins with the first angel's clarion call to worship God?

OLD TESTAMENT ASSURANCE

The Old Testament is permeated with the strong sense of assurance. Israelites had no question that God had chosen them and been gracious to them. Former slaves in Egypt living free in Canaan had no question that God had graciously delivered them and kept His promises to them. They also didn't suffer from a wishy-washy self-image that said, "Today an Israelite, but tomorrow? Who knows?" Strong national assurance led to strong personal assurance of their belonging to God. If anything, the Israelite was *too* assured. Messages of the prophets encouraged the Israelites to realize that they could lose their special belonging to God by persisting in sin.

Today many Christians suffer from the opposite problem—too little assurance. My own story told earlier shows I had that problem. I find many students of mine suffer from the same malady. They think it is wrong to recognize any assurance in their relationship with God.

Again it must be acknowledged that the New Testament *does* talk about assurance. Christians can have peace with God. We can praise God for our standing with Him on the basis of what Jesus has done for us. The Old Testament helps enlarge and fill out that picture.

Part of the reason for lack of assurance among Christians is an overemphasis on individualism. We have been taught to see ourselves as acquitted in court and declared not guilty as individuals. We are freed slaves—individually. We are forgiven our individual sins. While to a certain extent this is true, the Old Testament can help us also see ourselves as a part of the family of God throughout the ages—as adopted into a secure and loving group—the people of God. If we can see ourselves as parts of Christ's body, it can help us have a sense of the assurance of belonging—really being a part of things. That strong Old Testament corporate sense can assure us of our place. This strong group sense helps us see that it is not easy to leave a family or a tightknit group. One error doesn't expel a person. Only long-term, persistent evil finally puts one outside the group. The same is true of God's family also. The Old Testament can remind us of that.

Continued study of the Old Testament can promote both increased understanding and experience of the grace of God. When the whole Bible can be seen as one vast orchestra playing the symphony of God's grace with diverse instruments but with one glorious harmony, the music becomes even more rich and powerful than the music of a single instrument with a single movement played by itself. May this book contribute to that symphony.

> O Israel, put your hope in the Lord, for with the Lord is unfailing love and with him is full redemption. He himself will redeem Israel from all their sins (Psalm 130:7, 8).